Praise for *Astride*

"The world has long recognized the special bond of affection between women and horses, but less well known is how this bond has provided women access to traditionally male-dominated pursuits in sport, politics, and the workplace. With her deft writing style and impressive use of language, Eliza McGraw discusses in well-researched detail how the woman-horse connection has led to significant change in these areas and others. The result is *Astride*, a work that both educates and entertains—though not necessarily in that order."
—Mark Shrager, Dr. Tony Ryan Book Award–winning author of *Diane Crump: A Horse-Racing Pioneer's Life in the Saddle*

"Thoroughbred racing enthusiasts who enjoyed the deft and deeply researched historical flourishes of McGraw's *Here Comes Exterminator!* will be drawn in by her revelations in *Astride*, which shines a light on women whose long-forgotten accomplishments predate a number of generally accepted 'firsts' in the sport."—T. D. Thornton, author of *Not by a Long Shot: A Season at a Hard-Luck Horse Track*

"*Astride* weaves together horse history with the inspiring stories of trailblazing equestriennes. Through McGraw's blend of scholarly research and vivid storytelling, readers will encounter remarkable women—from pioneering suffragists and daring trick riders to devoted horse-welfare advocates, empathetic trainers, and more. Each page whisks the reader on vicarious adventures through the late nineteenth and early twentieth centuries, revealing how women partnered with horses to challenge societal norms or simply revel in the joy of riding. *Astride* illuminates the powerful bond between women and horses of the past, a connection that continues to thrive today."—Susan Friedland, equestrian lifestyle blogger at saddleseekshorse.com and author of *Marguerite, Misty and Me: A Horse Lover's Hunt for the Hidden History of Marguerite Henry and Her Chincoteague Pony*

"Eliza McGraw explores a little-known chapter of American history that has great resonance today. With fascinating anecdotes and rare period photos, McGraw brings to life the intrepid women who rode astride, challenging social norms and advocating for equal rights. This book is a must-read for anyone interested in history, horses, and American heroes."—Laurie Prinz, content director at Equine Network

"Heroines, horses, and history balance in equipoise in Eliza McGraw's fresh and superbly researched *Astride*. Readers, get tied on, because McGraw takes us on horseback in gallops through Central Park, off high dives from Atlantic City piers, and on fearless suffragette parades through the streets of Washington, DC. What a ride is *Astride*."—Josh Pons, two-time Eclipse Award–winning author of *Letters from Country Life*

"*Astride* excavates the way women on horseback shaped America in the nineteenth and twentieth centuries—and how America, in turn, shaped the horsewoman. In writing about mounted suffragettes, cowgirls, and circus riders, McGraw reveals a hidden history that stretches from New York bridle paths to the wild frontier. Her sixth book highlights both her research chops and a deep love for the American horsewoman."—Emma Hudelson, author of *Sky Watch: Chasing an American Saddlebred Story*

"Every woman who loves horses and sees them as an important part of her life should read this book. McGraw shows us how integral horses have been in the lives of American women, carrying them into equality over the past two hundred years. After learning about these pioneering female equestrians and how they fought to have the same rights as men within the horse world—and without—I can't help but feel even prouder when I'm sitting astride my horse."—Audrey Pavia, president of North American Trail Ride Conference (NATRC) Region 2

Astride

Astride

Horses, Women, and a Partnership That Shaped America

ELIZA McGRAW

Foreword by
Katherine C. Mooney

Copyright © 2024 by Eliza McGraw

Published by The University Press of Kentucky

Scholarly publisher for the Commonwealth,
serving Bellarmine University, Berea College, Centre
College of Kentucky, Eastern Kentucky University,
The Filson Historical Society, Georgetown College,
Kentucky Historical Society, Kentucky State University,
Morehead State University, Murray State University,
Northern Kentucky University, Spalding University,
Transylvania University, University of Kentucky,
University of Louisville, University of Pikeville,
and Western Kentucky University.
All rights reserved.

Editorial and Sales Offices: The University Press of Kentucky
663 South Limestone Street, Lexington, Kentucky 40508-4008
www.kentuckypress.com

Chapter 2 was previously published, in slightly different form, as "Belle Beach, Ahead of Her Time," *Untacked,* January 9, 2017. Chapter 4 was previously published, in slightly different form, as "The Premier Horsewoman of America," *Blood-Horse,* March 23, 2019. Material from both articles is reprinted by permission.

Cataloging in Publication data available from the Library of Congress

ISBN 978-1-9859-0127-8 (hardcover)
ISBN 978-1-9859-0128-5 (paperback)
ISBN 978-1-9859-0130-8 (pdf)
ISBN 978-1-9859-0129-2 (epub)

This book is printed on acid-free paper meeting
the requirements of the American National Standard
for Permanence in Paper for Printed Library Materials.

Manufactured in the United States of America.

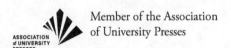

For Adam, Simon, and Macie

Contents

Foreword by Katherine C. Mooney ix

Preface xv

Prologue 1

1. Riding for the Vote 10

2. Urban Riding, Horse Shows, and Foxhunting 24

3. Women and Humane Societies 51

4. Women in Racing 68

5. Cowgirls 87

6. Circus Riders 109

7. Extreme Riding: The Girls Who Dared 124

Epilogue 141

Acknowledgments 143

Notes 145

Selected Bibliography 169

Index 173

Foreword

Katherine C. Mooney

I wasn't going to miss it. I always make a point of watching the Grand National, but the 2021 renewal felt particularly necessary. A few weeks earlier, Rachael Blackmore had magnificently dominated at the Cheltenham Festival, scoring five Group One victories and nearly snatching the Gold Cup itself. Now she had a live chance to become the first woman to win the famously testing Aintree contest. I was hardly alone, hunched over in a desperate crouch on my sofa. The racing writer Alastair Down admitted that, even though he had several close friends in the race, he was "roaring on Rachael," four fences from the finish.[1]

When Blackmore and Minella Times passed the winning post first, all the *National Velvet*–tinted dreams of generations suddenly crashed into reality. She wasn't a teenage girl, in love with a rambunctious rescue, who was content with a moral victory. She was a thirty-one-year-old professional who had seen her male peers, boys she had raced against on ponies as a teenager, glide to fame while she couldn't get mounts. Her old friend and housemate Patrick Mullins remembered the days when he and her boyfriend, jockey Brian Hayes, would head for the track and she would head to the kitchen to bake. "It was like her way," he said, "of punching the wall."[2] But she had gritted it out and forced her talent into the spotlight until she rode for the top trainers in Irish National Hunt racing. "Never mind her tactical awareness or strength," summed up the famously unsentimental horse owner and airline executive Eddie O'Leary. "She has bigger balls than any of the boys."[3] In 2022, she would win the one that had eluded her, storming with A Plus

ix

Tard up the Cheltenham hill to become the first woman to take the Gold Cup, as the crowd "made a sound worthy of a momentous occasion."[4] Hollie Doyle remembered a similar sound from the spectators after her victory a few months later in France's Prix de Diane made her the first woman to win a Group One European Classic race. Shocked at the crowd's joy, she suddenly realized, "what's just happened really."[5]

What had just happened was special, because it was an extraordinary feat that seemed on the brink of becoming ordinary. Female jockeys have occasionally won internationally significant races since the 1970s. They have topped American Classics, like the Kentucky Oaks and the Belmont Stakes; they have taken Breeders' Cup wins.[6] What we saw in 2021 and 2022 was not the first time women achieved at the top level in horse racing. But it was an indicator that more than one woman is at that level to stay, that others will inevitably and frequently follow. And what has happened in racing is merely the most prominent public example of women's achievement in equestrian sports. Since the 1950s, women have racked up Olympic medals on horseback, just as they have thrived for decades as professionals and top amateurs in saddle seat and Western disciplines. While women's sports have made tremendous strides in general in the last two decades, horse sports have an unusual distinction as one of the few forms of competition in which men and women take each other on as a matter of course. The best rider, the one who can command a thousand-pound animal with the most precision and authority, the one with the most well-honed balance and bravery? That rider wins.

But as compelling as that reality is, we mostly don't think of women and horses together in that context. We don't think of Rachael Blackmore; instead, we usually think of Velvet Brown, an ancestress of that type we often shorthand as the "horse girl." The horse girl can be an avid Instagrammer, her captions full of jokes about hay in her hair. She can be a reader of the myriad self-help and quasi-mystical books that attribute healing and empowering properties to horses. She can be an animal lover who always wanted to pet a horse but never could because of allergies and so gives regularly to equine rescue. She can be a woman who rereads *National Velvet* or *The Black Stallion* every year. She can be a teenager who rejects the strictures of young female gender performance and prefers the companionship of animals. She can be a six-year-old who draws a pony on her school pencil case. The scholar Ulrich Raulff could finally say only, "The 'horse girls' are a special case, a world unto themselves."[7]

What makes a horse girl is self-identification. And it is, undoubtedly, a privileged role. Being a horse girl with an actual horse entails discretionary income and time that can be devoted to something purely for pleasure. Even absent the real animal, it demands the resources to donate to the causes, buy the merchandise, risk the teasing. And the teasing is real. Like many forms of women's popular culture, being a horse girl often elicits affectionate or not-so-affectionate scorn. What a waste of money and time, what an irritating phase that should be left behind in adulthood. Even if we acknowledge that the role is inherently a privileged one, one for girls and women who have some space for choices, that can't be an excuse for dismissing it or them. Speaking as a lifelong horse girl, I always cherished the relationship I built with the animals, particularly because I was a young woman who did not feel accomplished at the usual rituals of girlhood. In my thirties, I realized that being on a horse was liberating because it meant living absolutely in the moment, thinking only of the partnership with the animal as we worked together to accomplish something. When I was forty-one, cantering a new and not-too-tractable horse around a small ring, my trainer said, "Okay, just give a little and let her carry her own weight," and I nearly laughed. My life seemed to be a constant series of relay races in which I carried everyone else's weight, and the very thought of trusting this creature to do it herself was intoxicating. Being on a horse became a tiny vacation from the obligation of taking care of others, from the assumption that I would be the one to remember all the details, prevent or soothe any hurt feelings. I can tell you that setting that down, even for half an hour at a time, is life-altering.

When I found out that Eliza McGraw, one of my favorite authors, was writing a book about women and horses at the turn of the twentieth century, I was delighted to be asked to provide a foreword. In these pages, you'll find what I think of as the horse girl's prehistory, an era when women turned to horses as their world was changing around them. Today's horse girls—and professional equestrians—are descendants of these women, and they will recognize themselves in these pages, but they will also see just how much these women did and how much horses did with them to make the struggles we wage today possible.

When we go back to the turn of the twentieth century, looking for images of women, we can find them trussed up in high-collared blouses or drowning in voluminous skirts, peering out from under imposing hats and staunchly impassive before the long exposure time of the camera. They sometimes seem as if they truly were sepia, as if their whole world could be summed up in those gray and brown shades and in the restrictions that sought to prevent them from living their own lives. Supreme Court Justice Joseph Bradley, writing to reject Myra Bradwell's attempt to secure a law license in 1873, proclaimed, "The natural and proper timidity and delicacy which belongs to the female sex evidently unfits it for many of the occupations of civil life. . . . The paramount destiny and mission of woman are to fulfill the noble and benign offices of wife and mother. This is the law of the Creator."[8] Women like Myra Bradwell would just have to bend before that divine truth. That timidity and delicacy barred them from most occupations outside the home would have been news to the immigrant girls and women who labored in places like the Triangle Shirtwaist Factory or to the Black women who flowed into cities like Chicago in search of jobs or to those who worked the fields of the South and West. But all women knew that their bodies were the subject of constant scrutiny, that they would not necessarily have control over even the most intimate choices of their lives. They all knew that their labor would not be deemed worth as much as a man's or even, often, labor at all.

Women of all classes and races would march and speak and organize for suffrage, and that was a dangerous choice. A suffragist protester, attacked at the march for voting rights timed to coincide with Woodrow Wilson's inauguration in 1913, begged for assistance from one of the policemen on duty. "If my wife was where you are," he snarled at her, "I'd break her head!"[9] But even if women faced danger together, they faced it differently. That parade, one of the most famous public expressions of the American women's suffrage movement, headed by the ethereally beautiful Inez Milholland astride a white horse, was racially segregated. Some women worked for the vote because they wanted the freedom to express their convictions, others because they hoped to force changes to public policy, others because they believed suffrage for women would be a necessary step on a path to universal suffrage and civil rights for all people. Still other women spoke against the right to vote, precisely because they feared that gaining the ballot would mean the removal of privileges and protections that they equated with safety and fulfillment.

And beyond the fight for the vote, things got really complicated. Voting was only part of the change women saw as possible at the turn of the twentieth century, though we now usually talk about it as if it were the whole of what they wanted, the magic rite that would fix everything. That was not how women at the time saw or experienced their situation; what they were fighting for was what the activist Marie Jenney Howe would call the right to be "not just our little female selves, but our whole, big, human selves."[10] That credo had as many meanings as there were women, and there was no single movement or philosophy that would encompass all of them. But they involved new understandings of women's bodies, new fields for them to work in, new vistas of ideas to think about, new responsibilities to take on and old ones to relinquish, new conceptions of love and commitment, authority and power, virtue and integrity. Just to try to describe all of what was in flux is impossible, let alone to explain what it all felt like.

This book doesn't try to make sweeping statements about how all women in that time thought about what was new and what they hoped for or feared. Instead, its lens refracts, illuminating women who were rich, poor, eastern, western, white, Black, urban, rural, satisfied, and yearning. It resists categorization and instead shows us the very richness and difference of these women's experiences so that we can understand more deeply how complicated what they were living through really was. What draws the women in this book together is that they had particular companions with them in their journey through a changing world.

In 1894, a reporter at the *Kentucky Live Stock Record* assured readers, "A woman is no longer in bad form because she talks horse; she is supposed to be up on the subject, and society smiles approval on her for so doing."[11] That writer was talking about the city women who attended horse shows and the races, who rode and drove in parks, in contravention of older ideas of gentility. Only a few decades earlier, a male medical writer had insisted that riding "produced an unnatural consolidation of the bones of the lower part of the body, ensuring a frightful impediment of future function, which need not be dwelt on."[12] As horses became less identified with labor and more with leisure, they retained their literal ability to carry people farther and faster than humans could go on foot and their metaphorical status as symbols of possibility.[13] Both their physical and metaphysical capacities mattered in their relationships with the women of the early twentieth century. Women who had always ridden precisely because horses were work animals continued doing so and displayed their prowess with them in ways that demonstrated just how capable women could be. Women who before would have been discouraged from riding became fierce equestrians, and women who had been denied the right to advocate publicly took up the cause of horses and their welfare and dignity. Not all these women technically rode astride, in the sense that their legs were on opposite sides of the horse. But they were all astride in the sense that they partnered with creatures who accompanied them into a future that seemed to have more possibilities than women had imagined even a few years before.

Those possibilities were in some ways easily quantifiable: the right to travel, the right to earn, the right to vote. But they were also in many ways deeply individual and difficult to define, because they involved how it felt to be both a woman and a person. This book captures moments in which women expressed what that meant to them, moments that speak to us directly even now. When a reporter asked breeding farm manager Elizabeth Daingerfield if she ever felt the need to have a male partner to run things, she explained that, no, she generally just handled everything. "I feel myself frightfully necessary, you see." It was a gentle way of reminding him that she was the expert in the conversation and how much that expertise was part of who she was, of how she understood and valued herself. In the West, the champion cowgirl Mulhall sisters drew the attention of a reporter who observed, "The girl who rides horseback has but herself to please." What a revolutionary idea for a woman, then and now.

When Elizabeth Cady Stanton made her case for women's suffrage before Congress, she boiled her reasoning down to a very simple idea. Women, she said, like all people were individuals; their lives were, for good or ill, their own. She called for expanded opportunities for the American woman, "the most enlarged freedom of thought and action; a complete emancipation from all forms of bondage, of custom, dependence, superstition; from all the crippling influences of fear. . . ." The result of that emancipation would be "the solitude and personal responsibility of her own individual life."[14] Women must have the right to face the world alone, and that was inspiring but also potentially overwhelming, a task in which no other human being could go quite all the way as a companion. But, as this book makes clear, the women of Stanton's time and ours are not completely alone. We have horses.

Preface

In the years from 1890 to 1925, American women rode horses. Many pioneered, taking their places among the first women to manage Kentucky stud farms, play polo, and ride bucking broncos. They played basketball on horseback, floated mounted beneath air balloons, held jousting competitions, and jumped horses through flaming hoops for whistling, cheering audiences. Some abandoned sidesaddles and rode astride. Others flaunted tradition by catch riding for money or tearing across open country on foxhunters.

"The desire to attract attention often induces women to ride," intoned an 1892 riding manual.[1] And horsewomen did draw attention but not through coquetry. Women of the era dared in general, risking their bodies and staking their places among athletes. Many of these endeavors bore an equestrian stamp, as women rode bicycles downhill at speed, straddled motorcycles, and piloted airplanes in breeches and boots. An elemental connection to horses tapped an age-old power that had belonged to knights and soldiers.

"Do women just really love horses? Or do horses love women?" writes contemporary endurance rider Lara Prior-Palmer. "Riding has offered a counter-existence to women since before the times of Lady Godiva or the Amazons of Scythia, one in which we can be demanding and assertive."[2] In the "counter-existence" of the late nineteenth and early twentieth centuries, tableaux vivants no longer satisfied. Instead, women rallied the petticoat cavalry and rode bucking broncos, remaking femininity to include equestrianism.

All of this took place during a very horse-focused time in America. There were 130,000 horses in Manhattan alone in 1900, or 26.4 humans per horse.

They mainly carried men, including police officers, park riders, and cowboys. Theodore Roosevelt brought the cult of horses with him to the White House, where he had the stables retrofitted to his specifications. But as the twentieth century began, many men ceded horses to cars. Celebrities like Alice Roosevelt Longworth and Helen Keller, along with cowgirls, circus riders, hunt-seat instructors, and debutantes, claimed horsepower for themselves. Reporters filed riding-craze stories about Manhattan socialites shopping on horseback, women who rode hobby horses for exercise, women horsebreakers, cattle rustlers, and jockeys.

From the vantage point of the twenty-first century, the partnership of women and horses seems preordained. In fact, the image of the horse-besotted girl and her pony has even grown cliché. In *Farewell to the Horse*, historian Ulrich Raulff writes that as the world grew increasingly mechanized, horses were relegated to "a recreational item, a mode of therapy, a status symbol, a source of pastoral support for female puberty."[3] But at the turn of the twentieth century, that story hadn't been widely told. Enid Bagnold, for example, didn't publish *National Velvet* until 1935, and Elizabeth Taylor didn't play Velvet on-screen until 1944.

Unencumbered by the yet-to-come horse-girl myth, American horsewomen took part in the horse's golden age—the last half of the nineteenth century—and the arrival of the New Woman after the turn of the twentieth. Several of these women stand out. Wolf-slaying Lucille Mulhall became famous as "the first cowgirl." Beautiful, doomed Belle Beach, an author and businesswoman, taught New York to ride. Studious expert Elizabeth Daingerfield, who drove around the Kentucky bluegrass with a car full of dogs and a pistol, managed Man o' War, the greatest racehorse of all time. Daredevil May Wirth flipped somersaults on her circus horse Snowball, whom she believed was a reincarnated knight. Humane activists across America advocated for urban workhorses and installed water fountains for them. Annie Tinker formed an equestrian brigade during the suffrage movement. *Astride* tells these women's stories, and those of women like them: riders, tamers, performers, caretakers, and teachers who partnered with horses. Most of the women in this book are white, reflecting which narratives have been preserved and privileged, not that women of color didn't ride or spend time with horses. Many are from the upper classes and could afford lessons, board bills, and hunt club fees, but there are also many women here—riding teachers, barn managers, diving horse riders—who worked for a living, or who rode to keep themselves out of poverty. Still, they had plenty in common, namely, a devotion to horses and riding.

The horsewomen of the New Woman era found endless ways to work and play with horses: galloping over high plains, traversing thousands of miles, tending foals, competing for rosettes, marshaling parades. They were with horses in that most specialized form of accompaniment that only riders know, characterized by the longing that defines partnership with these animals—to go faster, higher, to move with increasingly joined motion. With horses, there's always more.

The New Women knew this well—I think often of stouthearted, category-defiant Madame Marantette, a rider who moved the puissance wall ever upward, rode everlasting laps during endurance races, and schooled for hours and hours until her high school horses could predict her commands and execute the most delicate sequences. "You can't confine yourself to one thing; you must do everything if you are going to be successful," she said in 1903.[4]

As a horsewoman, I think this makes sense. For the purposes of this book, I sorted figures into categories to create some order. But no matter what discipline we prefer, our experiences transcend boundaries. I thought of the humane workers, who saw relief and mercy in letting sick horses go, when I had to have a beloved thirty-year-old mare put down. In Maryland, where my mare Audie is boarded, horsewomen campaign for conservation, much in the way that suffrage riders did, using parades, visibility, and work alongside other interest groups. We thrill to others' horses at a show or a race, just reveling in the life of the horse, their presence among us, the way so many horsewomen did at Madison Square Garden or at rodeos. And we believe in the specialness of our own horses as distance rider Nan Aspinwall placed her faith in her Thoroughbred mare, Lady Ellen. Like cowgirls, we fall off, and we get back on.

Today, there is a rich and ever-evolving library of animal studies, sports studies, and equine historical studies. While this book covers many of the same topics as the texts produced by writers working within those disciplines, it isn't an academic treatise. Instead, it is a composite portrait of a moment in history, a way for readers to focus on and inhabit a crucial time for American horsewomen. Contemporary reports including newspapers, photographs, and books helped me understand what these women did and how they were portrayed. These are the images they would have seen, the writing they would have read. Some wrote their own books and articles. Some didn't generate much coverage—they may have only earned mentions—but I included them anyway because even snapshots add texture and detail. As a result, this book is purposefully eclectic, just like the American landscape it covers. Plenty of the subjects mentioned here didn't even ride astride, but it is in that spirit—the willingness to change, grow, and publicly perform something new—that the women portrayed here rode, no matter which saddle they chose.

I spent a couple of years researching this book. I read biographies, some published by local presses, others sent from historical societies or bought directly from the authors themselves. While on a fellowship at the National Sporting Library in Middleburg, Virginia, I worked with materials including the papers of Lida Fleitmann Bloodgood. I looked at the correspondence of Elizabeth Kane, August Belmont's breeding manager, in an attic on the Pons family's Maryland Thoroughbred farm. The Keeneland Library was where I learned the most about Daingerfield. And at the Library of Congress, I stocked my study shelf with periodicals, cowgirl accounts, and harness catalogs. Online, I read thousands of old articles and leafed through countless photographs. I downloaded images and works from collections based across the country, from Calisphere to the Kentucky State Digital Archives to the Library of Virginia. I looked on Pinterest for "vintage cowgirl" images. My computer staggered, bogged down with book-length PDFs of rodeo-riding accounts and veterinary texts. A stack of riding manuals teetered on my desk. There were horsewomen everywhere.

For photographs, I relied heavily upon the Library of Congress's extraordinary collection and trawled historical societies for pictures of figures who may seem incidental to the country at large but are important to their hometowns. (In many of these photos, horsewomen hold their reins with just enough tension so that the horses will hold their heads in a particular way, something we still do today.) Captions are concise so that these images can evoke the time and place they capture—wide browbands, roached manes—but also the timelessness of horse tending and riding. They've been selected to bring readers closer to the figures they illustrate as well as to many everyday often nameless riders. The profusion resulted in a gallery of depictions that is less-than-traditional but will, I hope, take readers into a time that smelled a little like harness oil and bran mash.

To gather all these figures and tell their stories, the chapters are sorted by categories of horsewomen, including cowgirls, humane agents, and suffragists. Some, like Emma Peek, better known as Madame Marantette, traversed categories. She was a long-distance rider, a jockey, and a circus performer whose accomplishments cannot be confined to one chapter, so stories about her—jumping a horse over seven feet, chatting backstage at a circus—crop up throughout the book.

The prologue introduces readers to the era, with an accounting of the public debate over riding astride. Chapter 1 describes the mounted suffragists. With its inextricable link to society women, the suffrage movement offered an outlet for horsewomen who'd taken lessons in Central Park. They acted as the symbols in this most public moment, using Joan of Arc's image—armed, mounted, fierce—as a template. Chapter 2, which is about urban riding and horse show culture, returns to Central Park and other public, popular sites that hosted the turn of the century's riding craze. Rich women weren't content with piano and lawn tennis, and women like Belle Beach taught them to ride. Beach's theater of command, the horse show world of the early century, dictated the social seasons and raised sportswomen's visibility. Chapter 3 remains centered around the city, with a focus on the women who worked to ameliorate urban horses' working lives. They passed out nonslip chain horseshoes to teamsters in winter and straw hats to them in the summer. They lobbied for cab drivers to warm horses' bits and paced city streets searching for old and sick horses to pasture or put out of their misery.

Chapter 4 discusses the women who participated in Thoroughbred racing, which, along with boxing and baseball, was a primary American sport and a decidedly male arena. Trainers, jockeys, and owners smoked cigars, swapped tips, and drank in men-only spaces. Crossover between women in the show ring and Thoroughbreds kept the two combined; you might meet Astors and Vanderbilts at both. The exceptions took place farther afield, in places like Nevada, where a woman named Mrs. Bagwill rode; or Oklahoma, where Eliza Carpenter trained racehorses, ponying them alongside her wagon. Chapter 5 covers cowgirls like Annie Oakley and Lucille Mulhall. Like their circus counterparts, they showcased the power of women as performers, pushing limits with ever more daring stunts. Women (and there were more female bronc riders in the 1890s than there are today) competed against each other at rodeos in Wyoming, Montana, and Idaho. Cowgirls rode hard, mining the frontier space for a place they could outdo the grizzliest men. Chapter 6 discusses circus performers, whose gaudy flashiness embodied the flapper spirit. Alight with excitement and spangles, careening around the circus ring or a fairground, equestrian performers like "wonder girl" May Wirth glittered.

Athlete Eleanora Sears, ca. 1915. (Library of Congress, LCCN 2014701144)

Chapter 7 is about extreme riders like Martha Blow Wadsworth, who topped distance riding records on horses she'd bred herself. Diving horses plummeted from high boards into small pools before cheering crowds. Some diving horse riders went blind, their trauma a grisly consequence of risk. The epilogue moves very briefly back over the scene, because by the late 1920s, the partnership of women and horses grew to seem obvious to Americans, setting the stage for the familiar modern formula.

Astride could start many places, in this time when horsewomen captivated their country. But it seems fitting to begin in New York's bridle-path-laced showplace, Central Park, with what would become a very symbolic ride.

Prologue

At a livery along the west side of Manhattan's Central Park, Dorothy Chestick swung into the saddle of a rented horse. She adjusted her stirrups, picked up her reins, and entered the maze of paths. The light through overhead branches spangled the packed brown dirt. It was August 8, 1895.

The park was made for horses. Landscape architect Frederick Law Olmsted had laid out its bridle paths with gentle, canter-scaled curves, and they snaked and wound through leafed-over woods. Workers harrowed trails and stables lining nearby avenues leased well-mannered mounts. Cyclists pedaled along, their black dusters echoing riding habits. Shining carriage horses pulled barouches, victorias, and spider phaetons.

As Chestick, who performed in plays, trotted along, a policeman appeared in front of her. He said the way she was riding—astride, like a man—violated the law.[1] She should be riding sidesaddle, like the other ladies in the park. Chestick protested. What about the women on bicycles? They were certainly "riding astride."[2] But she was the scofflaw. Afterward, Chestick's manager contacted the authorities, and the park commissioners responded that an officer could apprehend any rider who was in an indecent position.

In those days, Theodore Roosevelt, who would not be president for six years, served as Manhattan's police commissioner. He said that Chestick had a perfect right to ride astride. The police needed to defend her, not cite her for scandalous behavior. "This new fashion in feminine equestrianism is spreading in this country, and what else could be expected when it has the

1

encouragement of actresses," scoffed one critic.[3] But the police assured Chestick that they would not stop her again.

She rode on.[4]

Chestick's story demonstrates the way people fought over the interaction between women and horses, usually because of what saddle was used. Many women rode sidesaddle, often seen at the turn of the twentieth century as the traditional and "correct" way for women to ride. Women who rode astride were referred to as Amazons, after the legendary group who rode astride through Scythia (today, Iran and parts of eastern Europe) in the classical era. "The celebrated equestrian expertise of steppe people, the centrality of horses in their lives, the nomads' own oral traditions, and perhaps a belief in a special relationship between independent women and wild horses led the ancient Greeks to believe that the Amazons must have been the earliest horse people," writes Adrienne Mayor in her study of the women.[5] Independence and wildness were not qualities that many Americans desired in women at the time. Harking back to the Amazons classed riding astride into something unrestrained and aggressive.

The sidesaddle, by contrast, connoted being ladylike, an appropriate way for a grown, settled woman to ride. It seemed European and elegant. You don't see Joan of Arc, for example, depicted riding aside. But riding sidesaddle also got women onto their own horses. They didn't have to ride double with a man anymore. Women jumped, galloped, and hunted, all in the sidesaddle. Plenty still ride that way today.

From the early eighteenth century on, a sidesaddle with two "horns" (not exactly like a Western saddle's horn, but a curved, upward fixture) grew common. By 1830, the "leaping horn"—a pommel that faces down—came along, meaning that the left leg now had some purchase, too. Lida Fleitmann Bloodgood, who will reappear later, and who wrote her own book about sidesaddle riding, called this invention "the horsewoman's Magna Carta or Declaration of Independence."[6]

Many nineteenth- and early-twentieth-century American horsewomen rode corseted on a horse's side, skirts flowing. They were astonishingly athletic and accomplished; riding a horse sidesaddle is not easy. Mule-bound pioneer women lurched up mountains in sidesaddles. Hunters rode to hounds that way too. Riding sidesaddle fulfilled Victorian-era norms because women who rode aside had to be helped on and off by a groom, trying not to flash an ankle from under their voluminous habits. As one writer wagged, this placed

Mrs. Delas Blodgett, 1919. (Library of Congress, LCCN 2016827237)

them "at the mercy of some man to begin with and to end with, and at the mercy of the horse from beginning to end."[7]

Some believed that Scripture forbade riding astride, because of a verse in Deuteronomy forbidding women to wear anything that "pertaineth unto a man." This meant that sidesaddle riding was "for modesty," a euphemism meaning it kept women from having anything between their legs. Many sidesaddle advocates hated the whole idea of women straddling a horse, and classified riding in a man's saddle as vulgar, medically unwise, and hypersexual. "Women Now Ride Astride," ran one headline, which had the ominous subhead of "Masculinity in The East." A woman who rode astride had "perverted taste," wrote one columnist. "We shall have some hearty fun at the expense of these Amazons," added another.[8] "It is all very fine to talk about [riding astride] being more graceful and more comfortable," another added, "until you have seen a woman sitting forlornly astride a horse, looking for all the world like a skewered bull-frog."[9]

4   ASTRIDE

Some reached for scientific explanations. "A woman has more of a grip in a side-saddle than in a man's saddle," said one instructor. "A woman's weight is mostly from the hips up. So the weight that would keep a man from being thrown in an emergency wouldn't be of the slightest use for a woman. Then, too, from the hips to the knees a man's leg is longer, consequently he can clinch the side of the horse and keep from being thrown in this way, while a woman couldn't, as the horse slants where her knee would come."[10] Even if you can keep track of all these clinches and knees and slants, this doesn't really make sense. But these explanations, from Deuteronomy to a bewildering parsing of anatomy, carried weight. Because of societal constraints, riding tomboy, clothespin, bloomer fashion, astraddle, man-fashion, or cross saddle—was for wild women with ungoverned appetites who craved speed, control, and danger.

Doctors could offer no "physiological reason" why women couldn't ride astride, one physician wrote in 1895. At the same time, he said, none of his colleagues would allow their wives or daughters to do it. There was no explanation for why they shouldn't. It just wasn't done.[11] Custom held strong, even for women who seemed otherwise transgressive. Outlaw queen Belle Starr rode through the West sidesaddle with a Colt .45 strapped to her hip. Annie Oakley, who shot guns for a living, performed trick riding feats from her sidesaddle, lying with her head on her horse's rump as she swept around an arena of admirers, her long skirt trailing.

Riding astride inflamed traditionalists as a "virtual license for ladies to wear male attire," as one columnist wrote. In November, the horsewomen of the North Side Riding Club in Chicago ventured into Lincoln Park wearing their divided skirts, sort of long culottes. With the voluminous draped fabric, onlookers couldn't always tell they were astride. Men stared and said nothing.[12] The daughter of Ohio Senator Mark Hanna dressed like a boy when she rode, so an observer needed to catch the chaperoning groom, or her mother following in a carriage to understand that she was a young lady in breeches.[13] Amelia Bloomer, who advocated for women wearing trousers, was enough of a problem, but who was to stop these Amazons from wearing their riding breeches all day?[14] Anyway, women in jodhpurs looked like "a lampshade on an urn," as one critic wrote. Women had stolen men's hats, coats, shirts, collars and boots, wrote one man, "but worst of all they have jumped astride of our saddle horses."[15]

Suffragist Annie Tinker (right) and a companion in their riding clothes. (Port Jefferson Village Digital Archive, John and Betty Evans Collection)

6   ASTRIDE

☙

Riding astride, according to one writer, "set the virtuous New York woman and the conventional riding-masters by the ears. They wonder how it must look! Last, but not least, they wonder how it feels!" In 1890, one instructor vowed that, "If any New York woman does try any such ridiculous thing, she won't try it in my academy."[16] "I hope shall never see so unpleasant a spectacle as it would be to see a lady riding astride of a horse," agreed another, continuing, "The men might like it. Without a doubt they would."[17] He did think it was all right for women to ride on either side of the horse. You needed two riding habits for that, and two saddles, but switching sides provided a "delicious sense of muscular pleasure." Why this proportion couldn't more reasonably have been found by just riding astride went unexplained.[18]

These men worked at big riding schools like Manhattan's Durland's Riding Academy, on Sixty-Sixth Street. Durland's catered to New York's elite families, with names like Astor, Rockefeller, and Belmont, and offered lessons to middle-class women who might not have their own stable. In 1890, a Durland's rider named Mabel Jennings fell off her horse. Convinced that the accident happened because of a cumbersome sidesaddle riding habit, she went to the riding school for her lesson on a Monday afternoon, when no one would be around, wearing a divided skirt, and mounted her horse astride. It was hard, she said. But she still felt that riding sidesaddle was wrong. Athletic endeavors, she felt, should be symmetrical.

"Seen from either side she looked like an ordinary woman rider mounted on that side from which the view was had," a reporter noted. "It was only when she was coming toward one or going directly from one, that the unusual impression was given of there being two ladies mounted on opposite sides of the same horse, of whom the head and body of but one was visible."[19] Jennings wouldn't say if she planned to try riding astride in Central Park. She didn't want anyone watching.[20]

The war over saddles raged well into the twentieth century. At a Pennsylvania horse show in 1911, organizers wanted women to ride aside. "Who ever heard of a man riding a side-saddle?" countered horsewoman Lucie Cherbonnier. "He would think you demented if you suggested such a thing."[21] (Not all women agreed with Cherbonnier. "I do not see any particular sense of women trying to ape men in their method of riding," said another.)[22] Meanwhile, a Georgia state legislator introduced a bill forbidding any girl over twelve to ride astride.[23] He had never seen a woman riding that way until he came to Atlanta. Circus riders—at least, if they were inside an enclosure—were exempt; their riding astride (along with their standing and somersaulting on horseback) didn't shock anyone. The bill made national news because women from around the country vacationed in Thomasville, Georgia.[24] The idea that sidesaddle was the only real way for women to ride lingered.[25] As late as 1913, a group prohibited women from riding astride in their parade.

The debate placed women in a socially and intellectually awkward position. Women were forced to take sides on something that did not need to divide them; some women rode both ways, depending on the day. Yet the question remained: What could women decide? How would they ride?

The specter of danger and the stated goal of increased safety hovered over the riding style discussion. The potential of grievous physical harm—especially when women chose it for themselves—challenged the idea that they required protection and physical safety. Riding means danger. The risk for every rider can be thrilling—that surge into a gallop, the moment a jumper's hooves leave the ground and you're airborne, defying the order of the natural world. Horseback riding is a leading cause of adult traumatic brain injury even today when certified helmets are available and worn. In the late nineteenth and early twentieth centuries, riding was even more hazardous. The press avidly covered horsewomen in riding accidents. A tragedy including women and horses always had legs, leaving us plenty of examples of what women riders signed up for, but also how they were seen, whether safe or harmed. The sometimes-traumatic results were all too real, and reporters covered these moments as if they were lurid crimes, detailing cracked heads and broken necks, a pony killed by a trolley on Atlanta's Ponce de Leon Avenue. One horse "threw its rider to death," when spooked by fireworks.[26] A girl was "thrown from a saddle horse and dragged thirty feet while out riding," when a bicycle went by.[27] A North Carolina woman screamed as a horse trampled her, but before people could rush to her "she was ground into a pulp by the forefeet of the frenzied animal."[28] In Washington, DC, a horse returned alone to his stable; his rider was found later in a patch of woods, her skull fractured.[29]

The female rider was typically faulted in these accounts. "I was thrown here and dragged and my arm broken, but it was my fault," explained one horsewoman in 1890. "My horse had been acting badly, and I had brought him down, when I lifted myself in the saddle to rest myself. He jumped and went out from under. My skirt caught; he dragged me and I kept my face clear by the tips of my fingers. Then as he turned the corner my hand struck the sheathing and one of his hoofs that had been flying back and forth in front of my face fell on my arm and broke it."[30] The rider blamed herself for her accident because she'd chosen to get on a horse in the first place.

In Chicago in 1911 a mare called Diablo ran away with her rider, who fell, her foot caught in the stirrup, and her head "beating against the pavement at every jump." The girl died when her body hit a tree as the horse ran by. One onlooker said Diablo had shied at a car and reared, and another said that the girl had lost her seat. He didn't believe her when she said that she could ride, the stable operator told a reporter, but she wouldn't pay for an escort. "We have had trouble lately with a great many girls from an amusement park, who come over here and tell us they are regular cowgirls. When they get on a horse we can see that they can't ride at all."[31]

Twenty-six-year-old Theresa Huntington Blake was from Boston and new to riding, according to a story in the *New York Sun*. She had started playing polo and riding cross-country in her sidesaddle. On a hot July day, she put on a gray riding habit and visited a stock farm near New Rochelle, New York, with her uncle, James Higginson. Blake looked over farm owner J. O. Holloway's string of saddle horses and picked out a bay gelding. Holloway hopped on his own champion jumper, Ben Bolt, and rode with Blake out to the cross-country course. Blake cantered around the field several times. Then, she steered the bay toward a jump that was about three feet high. His rear feet got caught on the top rail and he pitched forward, hurling Blake to the ground, then stepping on her chest. Higginson and Holloway raced to her as fast as they could, but her neck had broken on impact.[32]

Riders understand these harrowing narratives. Contemporary horseback riding, even for a beginner lesson or state park nose-to-tail trail ride, includes release forms, protective vests, and farm signs announcing horse professionals' lack of responsibility for death or maiming. The potential for death pervaded the way people wrote and talked about horsewomen, and the way they imagined themselves.

Women choosing to pair with potentially lethal horses flew against any lingering Victorian notions of women needing protection. The detail in accounts of riding accidents went beyond the common interest of readers in anything grisly to highlight the specific collision of women using horses to imperil their own bodies. The sheer fact of women doing something so

A group of women riding astride, 1923. (Library of Congress, LCCN 2016892185)

dangerous changed the conversation around them, making them harder to understand, both by men—even as they themselves rode—and to themselves.

On horseback, women could be bigger, louder, faster, and stronger—all qualities riding already offered men. Sometimes women wanted to ride sidesaddle. They just wanted to choose. "We are not trying to follow the ways of men in riding astride," said a Washington, DC, horsewoman. "We have just awakened to the fact that we are more comfortable riding that way."[33]

1

Riding for the Vote

In June 1913, British suffrage activist Emily Davison rushed onto the Epsom racecourse in Surrey, England. She carried two flags as the horses swerved, thundering for home. Bystanders wondered afterward if she'd hoped to pin one of them to the bridle of King George's horse Anmer, who was running full speed (probably about thirty-five miles an hour) when he smashed into Davison. She crumpled beneath his raking hooves and lost consciousness, rousing briefly to say, "The cause must go on," before dying days later.[1] Five thousand women joined her funeral procession.

The collision of suffrage with horses on the American side of the Atlantic was often less violent. Horses carried women in parades and pageants for a show of strength and heightened presence, and the women's suffrage movement caught energy from the optics produced by mounted processions. Activists burned giant watch fires in front of the White House and took women who'd been jailed on a prison tour, wearing their striped uniforms and riding in barred wagons. Horses furthered this highly visible mission, making women enormous and audible. The newness of a profusion of female riders, to audiences who lined the streets at some of the largest parades, showed that women were moving beyond asking for rights to demanding them, with animal amounts of noise and size.

Horses and riding entered discussions of the vote and equal rights, even in years that far predated the twentieth-century movement. "If woman considers herself the equal of man and capable of taking care of herself, she must give half the pavement if she does not want to be jostled; secure her own horse

Program from the Washington, DC, suffrage parade of 1913. (Library of Congress, LCCN94507639)

and help herself out of her own buggy," wrote an 1869 critic. "What a trial for a brave and masterly horsewoman, to dismount and secure her own steed?"[2] He could mock upper-class women—what lady would want equality if it meant she had to do a groom's job? But many American women did want to dismount and tie their own horses. They also wanted a say in their country's direction and future. So they took, mounted, to the streets.

The Senate defeated the first vote on women's suffrage in 1887, and in 1890 Wyoming, with suffrage, became a state. Colorado allowed women to vote in 1893; Idaho in 1896. By 1912, women marched for all. (National suffrage did not arrive until 1920.) "The uniformed women organizers on horseback demonstrated leadership and militancy, qualities usually gendered male; by their numbers," Mary Chapman writes. "Women marching in streets associated with their nation's government conveyed their collective power."[3]

Most women suffrage riders were white and privileged, able to afford access to well-schooled saddle horses and riding instruction, and the suffrage movement and publications of the time often ignored important Black figures, minimized participation of women of color, and marginalized women of lower socioeconomic status. New Women "held every expectation of political equality with men," writes Jill Lepore. "Quite how all this could be accomplished was less clear; apparently, equality with men required servants; much of early feminism was a fantasy of the wealthy, equality for the few."[4]

The movement emerged in a time of reckoning over how American women should appear in public. Suffrage activists inherited the preoccupations of the nineteenth century, when "studying the female body . . . offers a means of destabilizing the categories of public and private," writes Alison Piepmeier, "victim and agent, and other bifurcated ideals that have come to dominate studies of nineteenth-century womanhood . . . although often veiled with the costumes of domesticity, privacy, victimization, and proper femininity, these bodies were out in public."[5] Elevating women and increasing their physical presence, horses hoisted them into the open and onto the stage of the public streets.

Parades of the time were largely showcases for men—ethnic groups, soldiers, firefighters—so even planning a parade was a full-throated project for women. To resonate with crowds lining viewing areas, women transformed themselves into familiar mythological or historical figures. With their inheritance of a grandiose military feel, parades lent themselves forcefully to equine involvement. "Generals had ridden in parades on horseback to create a more marshal [sic] and dramatic atmosphere," wrote suffragist Rebecca Hourwich Reyher in her retrospective of the movement. "Women had not ridden in parades on horseback except back in the days of Joan of Arc, and Lady Godiva. We were creating our own mythology of women on the march, women active, and dramatic."[6] "Parades also permitted women to lay symbolic claim to the polity as they demanded the right to vote," as Holly McCammon writes. Riding down a city street together would prove equality in the most visible and tactical way and was "an important shift in the repertoire of collective action for the suffragists."[7]

"Suffragists," as Lepore writes, "didn't think Amazons were preposterous; they thought they were amazing. From the time of Homer, an Amazon had meant a member of a mythic Greek race of women warriors who lived apart from men."[8] Amazons partnered with horses. Their hovering image touched all the nerves—women taking what had been a men's privilege, women growing bigger, women making louder noises, women from whom you might need to run. Mounted women summed up the movements' goals in a dramatic, often splendid way.

Western rider Madge Udall rides in a divided skirt at the parade in Washington, DC. (Library of Congress, LCCN 2014692615)

The 1913 parade in Washington, for example, featured a troop of fifty "society women" on horseback.[9] With figureheads like activist Inez Milholland, parades showed that women who wanted the vote weren't hectoring harridans. Reporters even encouraged a debate over the greatest suffragist beauty. Milholland was first, and the runner-up was Washington, DC's Gladys Hinkley.[10] In their message and appearance, some women used what Milholland biographer Joan Lumsden calls "the eroticism associated with women on horseback. The parade's sexual undercurrent also underscored the risks women took in wielding beauty as a political weapon." A parade is public, alive, and festival-adjacent, as Lumsden writes: "The sensuality and carnival of suffrage spectacles always teetered on the brink of sheer frivolity."[11]

In February 1912, New York suffragists pleaded their case in the state capital of Albany. Horses were evident even in the earliest stages, when Annie Tinker told reporters she'd chosen the horse on which she'd lead a May procession in New York. (She picked her sixteen-hand Thoroughbred hunter.)[12]

Tinker riding at home. (Port Jefferson Village Digital Archive, John and Betty Evans Collection)

Tinker planned to ride with about fifty socially prominent women, including famous show rider and trainer Belle Beach. (More about Beach to come later.) "The young volunteer cavalry women have thrown away their stays, and donning riding boots and breeches, will this week begin training for the big pageant," wrote a reporter, using an either/or construction implying that horsewomen wouldn't wear corsetry, although plenty did. "Miss Annie Tinker, the beautiful young suffragist, who is arranging this extraordinary feature of the 'votes-for-women' demonstration, and who herself will lead the 30,000 suffragists down Fifth Avenue, was one of the first women to ride astride in Central Park," the article continued, underlining the link between voting, corset discarding, and riding astride.[13]

Tinker discouraged overdressing, asking participants to wear hats with a three-cornered "George Washington effect," partially so they wouldn't worry about their hair. "This hero business for men, I think, has been exaggerated to their credit," Tinker said. "Women, with all the sacrifices they make at such a time, and the hard work they do at home and on the battlefield as nurses, are absolutely left out when the laurel wreaths are passed around afterward." Mentioning Washington—and wearing his hat—Tinker was thinking along grand, historic lines. She would march not only for the immediate purpose but for a larger, president-sized impact. Milholland wedded her riding style to her activism. "I always ride astride," she told a reporter.[14]

Streets filled hours before the start of the parade at four o'clock on May 5. Most of the action was in Washington Square, and different groups flowed into their assigned different side streets. Marshals, wearing green and yellow sashes, directed traffic, and women held up signs—"A1," "B2"—to help marchers find their groups.

Grooms from a local riding academy led horses around the arch. May Bookstaver Knoblauch took charge. The horsewomen didn't wear uniforms. Milholland rode an overexcited, rearing bay, and by the time she calmed the horse, the other fifty-one riders were far ahead. Marie Stewart dressed, in chain mail, as Joan of Arc, riding a white horse.[15] The Old Guard Band blared out after the horses.[16] Women rode sidesaddle in riding habits, and astride in checked breeches. They wore derby hats and linen habits. Many favored black straw hats with the cockade of the Women's Political Union waving atop their crowns.[17] A thousand of the participants were men. Onlookers laughed at them, even the famous marchers like Rabbi Stephen Wise. A *Times* reporter noticed that the men didn't seem to know what to do with their hands.[18]

Assembling before a May 1912 parade in New York City. (Library of Congress, LCCN 2014692614)

An elderly woman rode, and a fourteen-year-old who handled her crop well. "Back to the wash tub!" a bystander shouted at them. "Who's minding the babies?"[19]

The next month, Ida Blake Neepler, dressed in another Maid of Orleans costume down to the chain mail gloves, rode a white horse at the head of a Baltimore parade behind a row of police officers—men in the streets had threatened to throw rotten eggs and cans of tomatoes at the marchers—and the chief marshal with her attendants.[20] A reporter noted that a soldier led Joan of Arc's horse, indicating that perhaps Neepler wasn't an experienced horsewoman but simply a game participant. The parade was in the evening—a little after seven—and her armor glinted under electric lights. She carried a silk banner adorned with a fleur-de-lis.[21] Six women rode behind, dressed in dark riding clothes with the purple-green-and-white suffrage sash over their shoulders. A band played.

Behind Neepler, the parade stretched a mile and a half. Six black horses pulled a black-and-orange float that commemorated Margaret Brent, an early

Inez Milholland. (Library of Congress, LCCN 2014691461)

suffrage activist, impersonated by a young woman alongside a man playing Lord Baltimore. Other horsewomen followed, and then floats representing the states that already had women's suffrage. The parade included Ben-Hur-style chariots representing Wyoming and Colorado, where women had the vote.[22] Maryland's chariot slunk behind one signifying free, victorious Utah. The Just Government League of Maryland, along with some supporters from DC, wore paper shackles.[23]

Parades like the ones in New York and Baltimore led up to the enormous 1913 parade in Washington, DC, the day before President Woodrow Wilson's inauguration. One of the movement's most vivid recorded images is of Milholland, mounted on a white horse named Grey Dawn, hair flowing down her back.[24]

The event marked the first time that women had marched down Pennsylvania Avenue and was also the first suffrage parade in Washington, DC.[25] Sixteen New York suffragists planned to walk to Washington for the parade, wearing brown cloaks and hoods, carrying leaflets and buttons saying, "Votes for Women."[26]

Activist Elizabeth Freeman poised to travel from New York to Washington, DC, for the parade. (Library of Congress, LCCN 2002712188)

Throughout the parade coverage, horses made news. "A troop of attractive horsewomen, known far and wide for its equestrian skill" or "a cavalcade of horsewomen," would appear, amid reports with horsey details—"cream-colored Arabian stallions," or Thoroughbreds who were "famous throughout the state."[27] The military language of male-centered parades dominated. One "petticoat cavalry" even called leaders "colonel" and "general."[28] During January, Baltimoreans readied themselves for the big parade in Washington with a "troop of attractive horsewomen, known far and wide for its equestrian skill."[29] A rumor circulated that Alice Roosevelt Longworth would ride.[30]

Inez Milholland, who would lead the parade on horseback in Washington, DC, was an activist, lawyer, and capable rider. Milholland was famous as the "most beautiful suffragette," and campaigned for the vote until she died at thirty in 1916. "Mr. President, how long must women wait for liberty?" she asked, moments before collapsing on a stage. Her husband went on to marry Edna St. Vincent Millay, who wrote a poem in her honor: "Only my standard on a taken hill / Can cheat the mildew and the red-brown rust." The image of the "standard" recalls Milholland's knightly horseback role.[31]

Milholland's wide allure lay in the fact that she "radiated newness, the totem of modernity," as Lumsden writes. She represented "the highest reach of the 'new freedom,'" as a contemporary reporter wrote, "as she goes riding a spirited steed down the street at the head of a demonstration, with her eyes flashing, calm, self-confident, but thoroughly feminine."[32] In this way, Milholland was, as Lumsden notes, the movement's "white knight."[33]

Most crucially, Milholland was willing to wear a flowing, eye-catching ensemble aboard Gray Dawn, tacked up in Renaissance European-style gear. Her getup evoked two famous and recognizable horsewomen: Joan of Arc, seen so consistently throughout suffrage pageants and parades. The other was Lady Godiva, often imagined as a beautiful show-off who rode naked. The legend reveals something quite different: piety, not exhibitionism, prompted that shocking ride. Godiva's unpleasant husband said he'd lower taxes on Godiva's beloved downtrodden townsfolk if she rode naked through the town.

Suffragist Alice Paul said that Milholland's raiment had symbolic meaning: green for hope, purple for loyalty, and white for purity.[34] These colors seem to be associated with Lady Godiva too. Alfred, Lord Tennyson's poem about Lady Godiva was famous at the time, and, as Milholland did, Godiva rides a palfrey, not unlike Grey Dawn, "trap't / In purple blazon'd with armorial gold." As late as August 2020, the purple and gold persisted; to honor the hundredth anniversary of suffrage, the St. Louis Arch was lit in these colors, explained as a combination of Kansas's gold from sunflowers and England's regal purple.[35]

Pageantry drew participants. In March, many travelers to Wilson's inauguration found closed doors because the hotels were booked solid with suffragists.[36] "Men Are to March," said one headline. Beneath that, a subhead ran "Shrewd Move by The Women." Army-trained women would ride in the "cavalry division." "These women know how to ride," a reporter wrote, in an account emphasizing equestrian numbers. "If there is any attempt to interfere with the peace and comfort of the marchers, these army women on their trained mounts will go to the front and do some 'riding down.'"[37] The descriptions offer some insight into the different types of contemporary horsewomen—that army-trained women or foxhunters would act as outriders to monitor the less experienced. Applause thundered for "General" Rosalie Jones, who appeared with her hikers in her brown gown to herald the procession. She carried red roses and a staff, a pilgrim.[38] Catcallers shouted and forced their way into marchers' paths. "Never in the history of the country has

Milholland with parade marshal Burleson. (Library of Congress, LCCN 2018661136)

the national capital been the scene of such a demonstration as was given here this afternoon when thousands of women fought their way inch by inch down Pennsylvania avenue [sic] through a mob of hooting, jeering men and boys, which the handful of police were unable to restrain," a reporter wrote. After an hour, organizers Lucie Burns and Alice Paul quite literally called the cavalry. A troop, stationed at nearby Ft. Myer, cleared the way for marchers; according to some accounts, the crowd (including participants) swelled to 250,000.[39]

Men spat on banners and tore them from women's hands. Milholland, "sitting splendidly on her horse," waded into the scrum.[40] "Miss Milholland represented the women of the future and as such gave a practical demonstration of what this sort of a woman can accomplish," wrote a reporter.[41] Along with police officers, Milholland—seeming at the same time an antiquarian icon and a woman of the future—rode into the crowds. At one intersection, she steered Grey Dawn into a wall of people, who stepped back. "You men ought to be ashamed of yourselves, standing there idly and permitting this

The crowd on Pennsylvania Avenue. (Library of Congress, LCCN 2014691485)

Riders in Native American clothing. (Library of Congress, LCCN 2014691441)

Milholland in New York, without the costume she wore in DC. (Library of Congress, LCCN 2014692616)

sort of thing to continue," she said. "If you have a particle of backbone you will come out here and help us to continue our parade instead of standing there and shouting at us." Men fell back and then began cheering at her outburst.[42]

Later parades learned from New York and Washington. In Chicago, Mrs. Charles W. Kayser chaired the horsewomen's battalion in the women's suffrage parade planned for May 2, 1914. She decided to ride her ranch horse Jack and sent out a call to horsewomen to meet so that she could assign them positions in the mounted battalion.[43] A midwestern version of Milholland would ride in a gold and white gown.[44] On April 16, the Chicago horsewomen gathered at the First Cavalry Riding Academy on 1330 North Clark Street. Some were experts, but others hadn't ever been on a horse before. One had to change horses because hers zoomed all over Clark Street. A marshal had to hand over her steadier horse, a chestnut named Chieftain, and ride the fractious one herself.[45]

In 1915, when asked why she was allowing her young daughter to ride in a suffrage parade, one mother said the girl could appear on the street as easily as at the Piping Rock Horse Show. The marching children—presumably of a class to attend society horse shows—were to wear white dresses with white sweaters and carry little green pennants in their "cavalry brigade." The leader would carry an American flag, and the riders, many on their own ponies, would wear uniforms with black derby hats and purple, white, and green sashes.[46]

They coupled their riding ability with the drive to seize the ability to vote, which would render women more powerful, visible, and dynamic, just like riding. The parades allowed them to harness the age-old, Amazon-reminiscent synthesis of horses and military might and display. We matter, the noisy hooves and attention-grabbing ensembles said. Look up. Look at us.

Many of these women had learned to seize attention already as urban and show riders. Because of their experience, they were at home on horseback on city streets, used to presenting themselves to the public—on bridle paths and in show arenas—from the saddle.

2

Urban Riding, Horse Shows, and Foxhunting

During the 1880s in Washington, DC, so few women rode horses in public that people would sing, "Lady on horseback / Can't count seven / Put her in a bandbox / And send her up to heaven." But by 1889, the sight of women riding through the capital was too commonplace for a jingle.[1] Similarly, in 1871, a writer longed for more riding in Manhattan's Central Park, since it was limited to "a riding-master, leading out his awkward squad for an airing," or "a lady and groom."[2] By 1890, however, there were twelve riding academies in New York, six in Brooklyn and Jersey City, and a few more in surrounding areas.

Mounting blocks—then called "upping blocks"—helped women get in the saddle without a groom's help.[3] Children learned to ride at around six years old, and riding teachers, grooms, and barn managers found work. Well-trained riding horses cost around $400, or about $13,000 today. Riding clubs held parades and rides.[4] Ladies' beginner classes, with one or two riding masters, often took place in the morning, with more experienced riders out in the afternoons. Women earned praise by handling "fractious" horses, appearing stylish, and exhibiting fearlessness and soft hands.[5] Shopkeepers stocked saddles, habits, hats, and gloves. The Manhattan Saddlery, which still stands today, opened in 1912.[6] The urban "riding craze" was officially underway.

The heightened interest in equestrianism meant that American cities, in which horses had long occupied space as work animals, increasingly offered room for recreational riding. New York's bridle paths saw wild action within their

Urban Riding, Horse Shows, and Foxhunting

Riding aside in Central Park on a horse with a docked tail. (Library of Congress, LCCN 2014688889)

manicured boundaries. Well-schooled police horses could stand for hours and then spring into high gear when police, forbidden to use lariats, caught runaways by galloping alongside.[7] Newspapers were full of accounts of riders handling tough situations. Nineteen-year-old Helen Van Hahn stopped a runaway one day in 1910 during her riding lesson. A horse, hitched to a small carriage, heard a wheel squeak on a trolley line and bolted, bouncing the driver out of the carriage while the passenger clung helplessly inside. Van Hahn grabbed the runaway by the bridle and held on; next, her instructor pitched in to stop the horse.[8] One very slushy day, a horse shied and bolted, and as his rider hung around his neck, a police officer rode up. "Keep away!" the rider shouted at the officer. "Don't touch him! Don't touch me! Let him alone, I can manage him." The horse slowed when faced with a giant pile of snow.[9]

In 1883, an expert horsewoman's mount bolted and ran from 110th Street and Central Park to 125th Street. The police officer in pursuit fell when his horse did. The first horse didn't stop until he reached a hotel's shed, and

Stereograph-mounted card of sidesaddle riding in Central Park, 1896. (Library of Congress, LCCN 2017649084)

his rider caught up with him on foot. She rested a moment, remounted, and rode off.[10] In one case, the rider, not the horse, broke a city ordinance against sidewalk riding by taking her horse right up to the door of a butcher shop. The butcher came out, smiled, and filled the written order she handed over.[11] A bloomer-wearing New York horsewoman named Hilda Johnson challenged a cyclist to a race. The contestants started at 84th Street and planned to go to 72nd and back. Johnson led, a police officer at her heels shouting to stop, and Johnson won by about three lengths, trailing a string of fellow spectator cyclists. The cyclist gave Johnson the ten dollars they had bet and moved off through Central Park with her friends behind her. Had Johnson ever ridden a bicycle? a reporter asked. "Oh yes," she said, "but I hate them. Give me a horse every time!"[12] In Washington, DC, urban riding meant First Lady Frances Cleveland handed out diamond horseshoe pins at paper chases—cross-country rides with judged obstacles—in Rock Creek Park.[13] Ethel Chase Sprague, whose father was a chief justice, coursed through broken branches and arrived, scratched and hatless at the finish to receive her scarf pin with rubies.[14]

Chicago "whips," or drivers, steered their phaetons along the lake.[15] Doubters believed the all-women Garfield Equestrian Club could suffer from infighting, but one reporter wrote that "it would be strange if women who were able to control their spirited horses, and that is not an easy matter,

City horsewomen in 1919. (Library of Congress, LCCN 2016827257)

were unable to control themselves."[16] The members did rate themselves above cyclists. Tire punctures, they pointed out, never ruined *their* rides.[17]

High style ruled city riding. New York women's riding habits were nearly uniforms: all dark and worn with either a high or round hat.[18] A Fifth Avenue jeweler filled an order for golden spurs. That wasn't rare, he told a reporter, though sterling silver spurs were more common. Luxury riding crops had gold handles or inset jewels.[19] In 1916, *Vogue* recommended that whether a woman was riding side or cross saddle, her skirt shouldn't be too full: "The apron skirt is the best; it is cut so that when one is on the horse the skirt comes over the side but only the breeches touch the saddle. When one dismounts, the skirt is buttoned over."[20] Famous rider Belle Beach believed that if the saddle fit well, you shouldn't need saddle pads except as a stopgap measure while you waited for the saddle fitter. All leather should be plain, she said. Monograms were "out of place."[21]

28 ASTRIDE

Horses themselves even came in and out of fashion for women as much as riding clothes and tack. Common city mounts included German warmbloods and mustang crosses. You might even see a branded western horse under English tack.[22] People disliked riding gray saddle horses, but seal brown and blood bay were popular. And while people had cared in the nineteenth century about a gait called the pace, by the early 1900s, this no longer mattered.[23]

Away from the northeastern corridor, horsemen mocked citified Easterners, whom they believed leaned back too far, only rode horseback to lose weight, and looked ridiculous in their too-tight corsets.[24] "There is no more persistent devotee to the new craze than the older woman and the fat woman," reported the *Chicago Tribune*.[25]

Astonishingly, the riding craze even extended to women who couldn't afford horses. One 1907 article suggested that women could ride chairs around their kitchen to get exercise. They were supposed to kneel backward on a hardbacked chair and rock it back and forth until they became comfortable. "After a time the rider grows so skillful that she can rock in all directions, simulating a trot, a canter, a gallop, and even a rack, by throwing her weight from side to side, as well as forward and backward, and causing the chair to rock on two legs, and then on the other two," a reporter wrote.[26]

You could also ride a rocking horse to similar effect, according to the *Los Angeles Times*. Women dressed in bloomers and lined up at a gym by open windows. Music played, and riders switched "horses" as part of the class.[27]

All this riding (evidently, even the horseless riding) required instruction. In 1884, Elizabeth Karr's *The American Horsewoman*, a riding manual and informational compendium, was, as one review stated, "the only book on the subject we know of."[28] The book, published by Houghton Mifflin, sold for two dollars. A reviewer found it overly basic in spots—for example, Karr advised that riders who want to turn left shorten their left rein—but also called it "primer and catechism as well as textbook and treatise all in one."[29] The *New York Times*, while agreeing with Karr that all riding schools should have at least one female riding teacher, quibbled with certain moments, for example, when Karr recommends that riders place a hand on a groom's shoulder when mounting. (Too familiar.) Also, the *Times* reviewer said, Karr didn't add special instructions for foxhunting, which is one of the best ways for women to learn to ride without fear.[30]

At a stable in Washington, DC, young riders started instruction with a wooden horse. For the first lessons, instructors rode with students, side by side, at a walk. After a few lessons, horses walked in a vacant lot, so that the rider learned some control. Next, they trotted, with an instructor teaching posting by calling out, "Rise on my count—one two three, four."[31] The same instructor said that women shouldn't ride astride because they overused the stirrups for balance while men gripped with their thighs.[32]

In Boston, two riding schools did most of the teaching. Then as now, riding lessons were expensive, and students came from costlier neighborhoods.[33] An indoor arena at a Baltimore riding school, used by many members of the hunt during the winter months, attracted attention, especially once astride riding classes began. Public viewing wouldn't be allowed until riders could post.[34] By 1909, Chicago women could choose among livery stables. One specialized in horses that allowed women to "lead the western life free and untrammeled," without English or high school riding.[35] In Louisville, an increasing number of women took lessons from riding master Harry Westerberg, who said he could teach someone to ride in six to eight weeks with three lessons a week. He didn't think women would start riding astride in town, he said, even if they rode that way out in the country.[36]

Women riders needed women teachers, some believed. For one thing, they were the only ones who really knew how it felt to ride sidesaddle. "A man or boy may learn to ride by practice; that is, he may tumble off and on until experience not only gives him confidence, but security and even elegance. It is not so with a woman," one instructor said. "Her seat is artificial; she must be taught how to keep it . . . [a man] cannot teach her to sit in the saddle, because he cannot sit in it himself."[37]

Others thought women naturally had softer hands than male riders and were thus more sensitive. There were a lot of rules: women should hold their reins as if they were "worsted thread" and be able to pick up the correct lead at the canter.[38] They should "bend like a willow in a storm, always returning to an easy yet nearly upright position," wrote one instructor.[39] Women should be able to purchase their own horses, knowing, for instance, to pass over any showing the whites of their eyes, because they were likely bolters.[40] "If a woman is to go riding, no matter who may be her chaperon [sic], nor

Helen Blodgett, 1919. (Library of Congress, LCCN 2016827239)

whether it be in the park or the hunting field, she ought to know how to take care of herself," instructed *Harper's Bazaar*. "Not obtrusively independent, but with that modest, unassuming confidence which is the result of a perfect acquaintance with all that the situation demands."[41]

Manhattan riding academies and livery stables like Durland's and Dickel's stood a notch below more exclusive clubs. Some families leased horses from Durland's to take with them on summer trips, but mainly, hirelings paced the same trails every day, leading to an urban legend about two Durland's horses who broke loose one night and were found in the morning, trotting peacefully abreast unmounted on the Central Park bridle paths.[42] You could tell who owned which horses by their bridles' browbands: checkers for Durland's, blue for another stable, Claremont.[43]

The achievement of fearlessness—the gift that makes a horsewoman—was Lida Fleitmann Bloodgood's reason for being. She grew up in 1890s New

Young riders with their horses, probably in New York City, 1915. (Library of Congress, LCCN 93507038)

Riders in Central Park, early in the twentieth century. (Library of Congress, LCCN 2017649058)

Bloodgood. (Library of Congress, LCCN 2014704578)

York in a wealthy but nonsporting family. But she cadged a pony from her parents early on and went on to a horse-saturated life. After high school, for example, rather than walk with her class of Spence graduates, she foxhunted in Ireland.[44]

Bloodgood went on to become a writer and scholar. Her memoir, *Hoofs in the Distance*, offers a view into the fashionable equestrian world of the late nineteenth and early twentieth centuries. It seems, in her telling, a little like a small town, albeit one populated with Vanderbilts, Clarks, and Astors, as well as legendary riders such as endurance champion Martha Wadsworth, who appears in the extreme riding chapter, and style-setter Belle Beach. Rich women weren't content with piano and lawn tennis. They wanted to ride. Just reading the always-italicized horse names in Bloodgood's memoir evokes the cosmopolitan horse show world: *Flying Machine, Secuga, Rockbar, Confidence, Whalebone, Wathen, Cygnet, Judge Fulton, Lady Kathryn, Mr. Jorrocks, Greek Dollar, Hula, Northman, Palmetto, Bob Ryan, Dynamite, Longwood,* and *Golden Duck.*

For twenty-two years, Bloodgood rode at her "second home," the Gentlemen's Riding Club of New York, a place with separate carpeted parlors for ladies and men, more exclusive than Durland's or Claremont. Here, sugar bowls stood on the furniture. Members' instructions transmitted via teletype to the manager. Magazines like *Bit & Spur* and *Country Life* were available only in the men's parlor, but Bloodgood would filch them when she could.

Bloodgood took lessons in a sidesaddle "as deep as an armchair, [with] long hooked pommels and a stirrup-leather on a roller, that, serving also as balance strap, could be lengthened at will from the saddle on the off side," as she writes. Children rode in Central Park on Wednesdays and Saturdays, under the watch of an English riding mistress, who "needed but a few more inches of flowing skirt and veil to be an exact replica of the eighteenth century 'Lady on Horseback' prancing across an old print in the Club."[45] There were "rough-riding" classes and tent pegging when the weather was too icy to ride outdoors.[46]

A young woman's day at the club might start with twenty couples—one riding and one driving, all in white buckskin harness—performing a complex quadrille for a club audience. Next, she'd "ride gaily through two succeeding drills, change into a ball-dress, eat a five-course banquet offered by the Tandem club, dance the Viennese waltz till dawn, and then without even going

Theodore and Edith Roosevelt riding through Washington, DC, in 1902. (Library of Congress, LCCN 2013651279)

to bed, get into hunting clothes and motor off for a day with the Meadow Brook hounds."[47]

Reporters chronicled the Roosevelt women's equestrian adventures—including foxhunting—as much as their patriarch's. When Edith and Theodore Roosevelt went out, they left the White House quietly in a carriage and then mounted their horses.[48]

Ten-year-old daughter Ethel Roosevelt made the papers in 1902 when her saddle slipped, and she almost fell off her pony. (Her father tightened her pony's girth.)[49] When she rode around Washington in divided skirts, a reporter noted that "Miss Ethel is her father's own child, respecting the riding of a horse. She was put at it young and sticks to it well."[50] Ethel's elder half sister, Alice, was photographed on her new mare.[51] A few days before her fifteenth birthday, Ethel was riding with friends when her horse collided with a car, shied, and bolted.[52] Later that year, she was thrown from the buggy, and that horse bolted too. (Roosevelt had posted signs forbidding cars within the gates of his estate in New York. That made for a quiet environment, but

First Lady Edith Roosevelt's mare at the White House stables, 1903. (Library of Congress, LCCN 2010645539)

cars then scared horses, who weren't used to them.)[53] People teased Roosevelt when he asked for spunky horses from Ft. Myer for his children and their friends, because they fell off and were forced to take the trolley home.[54] Ethel, too, fell off during a foxhunt in 1908 when her horn broke.[55]

There were many stories, but the strangest intersection of Roosevelt and women riders may have taken place in 1908. On a Thanksgiving Day ride in Rock Creek Park, a seminary teacher named E. I. Sisson was riding out with some of her young students when her group encountered the president's. She later said that Roosevelt told her group not to pass them, rode angrily by, and smacked one of their horses with his crop. The president's group had been riding so slowly, Sisson said, that they'd thought it was all right to pass.[56] When Florence Cribben, one of the riders, returned home to Chicago, she found a crowd of reporters waiting for her. She didn't talk. Given Roosevelt's position as the patron saint of riding and great encourager of women on horseback, this was a strange incident. The idea of him as cranky, let alone violent, while on a horse surprised Americans.

Weeks went by and several articles were published about the incident; the president's secretary said that, like Cribben, the president had no comment.[57] Then, Cribben changed her mind. She told reporters that the president hadn't hit a horse, although Ethel Roosevelt did lecture them.[58] Meanwhile, the mother of May Rhodes, the rider whose horse was reputedly struck, wrote a letter saying none of it happened. She wanted the White House to deny the story too.[59] "I am glad to hear from you that your daughter denied the story that I struck her horse. Of course, I never struck her horse or any other lady's horse," Roosevelt wrote back.[60]

Here was what passed for a racy horsewoman joke: An accomplished rider was asked if she rode bareback occasionally. "No, sir!" she said, "when I ride I always wear a suitable wrap!'"[61]

Riding lessons and urban park riding offered ease not only while women rode along bridle paths but while they rode in horse shows, which were often elaborate affairs with multiple classes in a long day of exhibition. Shows offered upper-class women a place to exhibit what they'd practiced and a focus to a social season. By 1898, there were more American horse shows than in any previous year, and by 1909 women were in nine of ten classes at the Riding and Driving Club show in Brooklyn.[62]

The New York Horse Show, held in Madison Square Garden, was the largest and most formal of these events.[63] "Mrs. Alfred Vanderbilt, Miss Hopeton Atterbury, the Military—a few horses, a Roman background—that's the Horse Show," said one article. (The Vanderbilt driving team horses were named Venture, Vanity, Viking, and Vogue.)[64] Riding in a ladies' hunter class or driving four-in-hands was how an upper-class horsewoman demonstrated her skill while others, bedecked with jewelry, watched "the tanbark" (the mulch-like substance that was used for the footing of horse show rings) from boxes.[65] In 1909, a reporter used "women whose names frequently appear in the list of entrants at horse shows," as shorthand for society ladies.

The ramp in Madison Square Garden smelled, Bloodgood wrote, "of tanbark and sawdust, horse, dog, elephant, lion, peanut and orange peel." Her typical day during horse show week was spent "exercising a horse in a crowded ring, where hackney ponies, five gaited 'saddlers' and jumpers

A competitor in a driving class in a horse show. (Library of Congress, LCCN 2014682975)

fought for right of place; at noon a quick snack of Sanatogen [a sort of tonic] at the drug-store, or luncheon with the big hats of the show at the Prince George Hotel of Café Lafayette, followed by a tense competitive afternoon and evening—and perhaps a great win, and champagne drunk from a silver trophy at the Waldorf."[66]

In 1915, Bloodgood was riding her lightweight hunter, a gray mare named Cygnet, in a horse show. The footing was so muddy that show grooms had thrown hay around the obstacles to add some traction. Bloodgood had piloted her bay gelding over the jumps, but when Cygnet faced a brush with a white rail on top, she fell, pinning Bloodgood beneath her and fracturing her right leg in two places. A nearby doctor tore some sticks from the jump for a splint.[67] The judge asked that she be moved while she waited for the stretcher so the show could go on.[68] She attended that year's Madison Square Garden horse show in a wheelchair.[69] "Although I would naturally have preferred being in the saddle," she wrote, "I confess to enjoying the commotion."[70]

A 1903 cartoon showed spectators, judges, and horses all craning toward Alice Roosevelt in her horse show box. (Her father despaired of her love for

Madison Square Garden, 1909. (Library of Congress, LCCN 2014681654)

equestrian society functions; he liked riding as a more outdoorsy pursuit.) Magazines like *Horse Show Monthly* chronicled who went to which shows and which entrants won. Belle Baruch, a famous show rider, went on to compete internationally later in the 1920s, one of the first women to do so.[71] Even with the frivolity surrounding it, riding was serious. New York riding teacher Emily Beach explained once that riding encouraged empathy because "a girl who looks into a horse's face and into his honest eyes will be a better girl and a truer woman."[72]

Not all riders were, like Bloodgood, amateurs. Chicago horse show rider Ellen Rasmussen, who wore jockey silks under a knee-length coat, worked all over the country.[73] At a show in Pittsburgh in 1910, she and fellow professional Helen Prentiss rode all except one horse entered in the ladies' hunter class.[74] "I will never marry again," she said after her divorce. "I love my horses too well to let any man come between them and me in the future."[75]

Riders stayed busy. A typical day of classes at a New York Horse Show might include draft horses shown to halter, novice harness horses, Thoroughbred

Riders at the Plainfield, NY, horse show in 1908. (Library of Congress, LCCN 2014680565)

saddle horses registered in the studbook, appointment class, ladies' qualified hunters, and four-in-hands.[76] At a show in 1911, fresh flowers perfumed the air, and mounted police performed, galloping twelve abreast, then suddenly stopping to wind into a formation of smaller and smaller circles to whooping cheers.[77] Ring grooms wore pink coats, and spectators—in ermine, diamonds, and lace collars—leaned over the rail, others pressing behind them to see.[78]

Newspapers covered shows all over the country. A 1902 Indianapolis horse show had grand, Madison Square Garden ambitions. It was to be housed in a temporary amphitheater which had ninety boxes looking down on a tanbark arena. Flags and thousands of colored bulbs, in show colors of green and white decorated the area, and the governor and mayor made introductory remarks.[79] In Los Angeles, horse shows included more western-themed events, like a day devoted to a "tournament of cowboy sports." Later, riders performed a mounted Virginia reel to gramophone music.[80]

"It does not take me long to make friends with a horse," twenty-year-old horse show champion Belle Beach told a reporter in 1900.[81] That was an understatement. Beach could hop on a horse she had never seen before, pilot him

Rider at a horse show, ca. 1910–1917. (Library of Congress, LCCN 2016853899)

A sidesaddle rider in a horse show, 1910. (Library of Congress, LCCN 2016863556)

sidesaddle around a course of high jumps, and win. She galloped horses in the hunt field, using cotton thread for reins. She taught riding, trained horses, and won more than two thousand blue and red ribbons over the course of her twenty-year career.[82]

Unlike many of the competitors of her era, Beach was not a debutante or matron. Instead, wealthy families like the Whitneys, Vanderbilts, and Harrimans paid her to soar over jumps and gallop hitched teams around sharp corners at shows. She was hailed as America's best horsewoman. Beach's mother, Emily Beach, taught riding in Manhattan, and Belle was raised against a backdrop of Gilded Age wealth and style. An 1894 newspaper article positioned Emily Beach as the first riding teacher who catered to women. Emily Beach wouldn't tell the reporter how much money she made, but she rented an entire floor of an apartment building, owned a Great Dane and an Angora cat, and gave parties for her young daughter. Beach, the reporter noted, was "as much a member of society as any one [*sic*] can be who is not actually put down in the calling and ball lists of McAllister's 400 [a society list.]"[83] Horses

Belle Beach. (Photo by Burton F. Welles; courtesy New York Public Library digital collections, b13117836)

were Beach's "profession, pastime, and passion, though it was not obvious by the way she carried herself like a true lady."[84]

At one Chicago show, Belle Beach won the combination class for riding and driving, which had twenty-eight entries. She was the only woman. A local reporter asked what she thought of the local horse show. Beach said that the audience shouldn't hiss at unpopular decisions. She wasn't impressed with how everyone looked either. Back home, she said, some of the competitors would have been sent away for their Western getups.[85]

At a 1903 Durland's show, Beach, riding a "magnificent" woman-owned black horse, beat department-store heiress Carolyn Ridley Gerken in the ladies' saddle class.[86] Gerken hated losing, even to Beach, whom she sometimes hired to show her horses.[87] Once, when Gerken only placed fourth at the Monmouth County horse show, she hurled the white ribbon to the ground and scratched her other horses.[88] In 1906, she rode straight out of the ring before the judge could pin a second-place ribbon on her horse.[89]

Often, however, Gerken took shows by storm; in one Philadelphia show in 1902, she won second showing her bay stallion, Doncaster Model, and then a blue with Mistress Nell in a class for cobs under saddle. She won two more ribbons in the afternoon, winning honors in the hackney and horses-in-harness classes.[90] In 1904, she won three firsts.[91] "Mrs. Gerken's

Horse show spectators, 1909. (Library of Congress, LCCN 2014683289)

Big Night," ran a headline in the *Times* that did not need to explain who Mrs. Gerken was.[92]

At Gerken's twenty-three-acre Long Island farm, Gerkendale, she bred saddle, harness, and trotting horses. She had fifty horses there. The airy barn housed a practice ring where Gerken broke her own horses to saddle.[93] A reporter took pains to assure readers that despite her energy and skill, Gerken wasn't masculine. One might "be excused for drawing a mental picture of her as an amazon . . . with the atmosphere of the stable clinging to her," the reporter wrote. Instead, the reporter continued, "Mrs. Gerken is not a bit 'horsey' in appearance or conversation." She exemplified the perceived positive aspects of equestrianism, since she was "delightfully feminine at all times; her voice is soft and musical; she wears dainty draperies when outside the practice rig, and there is nothing muscular in her physique, except, perhaps, her wrists, which are like steel."[94]

"Horsiness" was undesirable, leaving horsewomen to tread a very careful line. It was all right to have steel wrists or be an "intrepid" horsewoman, but being "horsey" had connotations of masculinity, including coarseness and even actual smelliness—the "atmosphere of the stable" could convey

Horse show, 1914. (Library of Congress, LCCN 2016865449)

familiarity with stableboys or the actual odor of hay and manure. The New Woman was strong, composed, and performed, sometimes, in a way that society considered "like a man." But to stay within bounds, she had to be, like Gerken, not masculine.

To see "a living example of perfection in riding clothes," wrote etiquette expert Emily Post, "go to the next horse-show where Miss Belle Beach is riding and look at her!"[95] Beach was "part of her horse, cool, calm, reposeful, perfect of seat and poise, guiding her mount by a telepathy of a clear, wise mind and light hand, rather than by physical strength and ill-advised generalship," reported the *Monthly*.[96]

Next to a piece Beach wrote for *Vogue*, a picture showed her standing, dismounted, in profile, wearing a snow-white collar, and a top hat with her dark hair gathered behind. She held a riding crop in a long black coat. Girls should begin riding at seven or eight years old, she said, and she did not care for the cross saddle. "The average woman is not built for this style of riding," she wrote, "for not only are her legs too short, her thighs too thick and her hips too big, but she is cushioned too high to enable her to keep close down on the saddle with the necessary firmness."[97]

In 1905, Beach (identified as "a professional rider") was showing a horse named Chappie Lee in a hunter class. She was, as always, riding sidesaddle, and the horse seemed to dislike something about her skirts. Beach was about to take the first jump when the saddle slipped and Chappie Lee bolted, slammed into a barrier, and ran headlong toward the fence that separated viewers from the ring. Nearby grooms tried to stop him by waving their hands, but there was a jumble of "rearing hunters, flying hoods, and excited men." Next, the horse ran toward the judges' stand and scattered the judges. He whirled, racing along until some of the helpers grabbed the reins and dragged Beach off the horse. Beach asked for another saddle. She got back on and rode three times around the course to applause.[98]

Because of her pioneer status, it seems odd that Beach clung to her sidesaddle long after many women switched to riding astride. "Women are not built like men physically, and do not and cannot get their grip on the horse in the same way," she told a reporter.[99] As late as 1916, she thought riding astride was a passing fad.[100] (She did think it was all right for her students to skip corsets.) Beach held some retrograde opinions. She didn't believe that tail docking harmed horses, for example. She said she'd seen many long-tailed horses get in accidents when their tails caught in the reins.

In 1906 Beach married William Charles Bain, a Boer war veteran who fought for Scotland. She met him at the New York Horse Show. "He was a fine horseman," said one article. "They fell in love quickly, and, it is said, Bain, who was a newcomer, was unable to do himself justice when showing because he could not keep his eyes off the young woman."[101] But by 1912, they had divorced—Beach charged nonsupport and rumors flew about a lover Bain had left in South Africa—and Beach went to court to retake her maiden name.[102]

That same year, Scribner's published Beach's riding manual, *Riding and Driving for Women*. It was dedicated, mysteriously, to a "friend," and opened with a Walt Whitman quote from his poem, "I Think I Could Turn and Live with Animals," which is about the appeal of the nonhuman parts of animals: that they are "placid," for instance, and "do not lie awake in the dark."[103]Beach's book keeps Whitman's sentiment in mind. Even with the sidesaddle recommendations, it's a prescient book, with sections that prefigure some of today's ideals. For example, a rider should control "her horse with

46   ASTRIDE

a spirit of love instead of adopting the brutal method of controlling him by fear."[104]Its horse lingo invites familiarity: "Equally bad is the horse with no mouth at all," Beach writes, meaning that a rider should be able to communicate with her horse through the reins.

Other sections deal with more minor details. "Never 'cluck' to your horse," Beach writes. "It is a very bad habit to acquire, and, when you are riding in company, the other horse or horses are sure to hear you and to increase their gait."[105] She warns against flourishing a whip and issued very clear ideas about turnout. Ascots should only be worn with a plain bar gold pin, drivers should always have a lap robe and only use a brown webbing girth if you are riding informally, in the country. Those dark girths, she writes, are "liked chiefly by lazy grooms," presumably because they did not have to be cleaned often, since they didn't show dirt.[106]

Riding and Driving for Women was well-reviewed and hints at the larger societal issues at play. It's easy to imagine Beach-the-suffragist when she writes, "if a woman and a man are both going to the same fence, she should not expect him to pull up and allow her to go over first or to treat her otherwise than as he would another man."[107]

Beach succeeded in her riding life for many years, but in the years after the publication of *Riding and Driving for Women*, she no longer won ribbons. Things slid downhill. In 1913, a storage company seized her possessions for nonpayment.[108] By 1914, Beach filed for bankruptcy. She said she owed the Harriman National Bank $875 and Mrs. Condé Nast $75.[109] In 1917, Beach was stopped on Riverside Drive after a car crash. She was accompanied by an unnamed man.

After that, Beach's name mainly stayed out of the papers until 1926, when she died, alone in her Great Neck, Long Island apartment. A friend claimed her body. She had been sick; there were rumors of suicide. "World's Greatest Horsewoman Dies, Forgotten, in Obscurity," ran one headline.[110] It was a sad and surprising end for a former celebrity who ushered in such a dynamic, exciting time for women and horses. As a working athlete, Beach occupied a crucial space in the show rings of the early twentieth century. Unlike her students and clients, she relied upon her riding for more than social status or exercise. As one of the first people to write a manual specifically for women, Beach helped revolutionize the idea of riding and riding instruction. Her fame led legendary high school trainer Tom Bass—the first Black person to show a horse in Madison Square Garden—to name his prize show mare Belle Beach.

Horse show in Washington, DC, 1915. (Library of Congress, LCCN 2016866385)

Beach never lost sight of the partnership at the heart of her work and life. "That which takes but a moment to tell has taken me years to learn," she wrote, "learned as a pupil; learned as a teacher; learned by observation; learned by exhibition, by many a triumph, by many a heart-break; much of it a pleasure, much a hard task, but repaid always by my comrades through it all—the horses."[111]

Foxhunting was not, of course, an urban pursuit, but city riders, including Beach, rode to hounds in suburban and rural areas near places like Philadelphia, or Washington, DC.[112] Beach wrote that ladies shouldn't expect any special treatment in the hunt field, because "a woman must expect to take her changes with the men, and she is not entitled to that courtesy and deference which she may expect on other occasions."[113] When riding with the hunt, losing your stirrup or hat didn't mean your male companion had to stop. You were allowed to wear monograms here because the initials of the hunt could be on the habit. Spurs, on the other hand, were "a cruel means of enforcing speed and not just the thing for a woman."[114]

Martha Hazard takes a wall jump in a show ring, 1911. (Library of Congress, LCCN 2016863575)

Foxhunters. (Library of Congress, LCCN 2016829481)

Doing tricks during a horse show in Washington, DC. (Library of Congress, LCCN 2003653741)

Women should mind how they entertained their fellow foxhunters, according to one article that advised serving sorbet in tiny buckets with silver horseshoe covers. Also, a lady should give the band at her hunt cotillion instructions to play songs such as "Drink! Puppy Drink," "The Place Where the Old Horse Died," and "A Southerly Wind and a Cloudy Sky."[115]

Meadowbrook's hunt was led by the "New York Dianas." This group included Emily Ladenburg, who rode often in Europe, and Eloise Kernochan, who liked to ride three days a week with Meadowbrook and kept a horse previously owned by the Duke of Marlborough.[116] The Chevy Chase Club, just outside Washington, DC's borders, owned thirty hounds. In 1901, member Daisy Letter bought two horses for $1,000 each, roughly $32,000 today.[117] Members' horses were stabled at the club, and riders met them, groomed and saddled, at the hunt field.

Horses gave upper-class women a way to act in public that included physicality, style, and authority. Horses became a vehicle for typically out-of-bounds behavior that included riding for suffrage rights, public competence, and pushed-to-the-brink athleticism. "Never will I forsake the horse for the wheel, or the golf sticks, or the oar or anything inanimate," said show rider Mary Algood Jones. "I predict that half the women who have gone golf and automobile mad for the moment, who have ever known the joys of horses will go back to the horse."[118]

Even women who enjoyed their companion horses so heartily had to understand that not all horses were pampered foxhunters. The cart, trolley, and firehorses they saw on the streets near their urban bridle paths deserved good treatment too. Their own pets luxuriated in stalls, eating oats and alfalfa, but horse-loving women rallied to the cause of the urban working animal.

3

Women and Humane Societies

Today, women watch out for horses. They retrain off-the-track Thoroughbreds for other jobs, found therapeutic riding centers, and raise money for the feral herds that roam barrier islands. The New Women did, too, focusing on the urban workhorses heaving and clomping through their everyday lives. Their efforts were part of a societal drive toward improving the lives of the voiceless. Helping horses was a way women could mold a more humane world for the lowest laboring animals, whose riding relatives they babied.

The nineteenth-century drive toward protecting workhorses began, legend dictated, one day in 1866 when Henry Bergh stopped a wagon driver from beating a donkey. The patrician Bergh became an activist. As many have noted, the original seal of the American Society for the Prevention of Cruelty to Animals (ASPCA) he founded depicted a female sword-wielding angel halting a teamster hitting his horse. The horse, who has fallen between the traces, looks at his hidden-faced abuser with blinkers covering his eyes, mouth agape in mute shock.[1] Like Bergh, many late nineteenth- and early twentieth-century American women animal welfare activists took on the role of that forbearing angel. Women worked with the Red Star society, the New York Women's League for Animals, the Anti-Cruelty Society in Chicago, American Anti-Vivisection Society, Women's Humane, Ryerss Infirmary for Dumb Animals, and the Red Acre Farm for Horses. Journals like *Our Dumb Animals* and *Humane Journal*, with women-authored articles, kept activists informed.

In any American city at the end of the nineteenth century, you could buy straw horse hats, padded collars, special winter shoes, and ventilated nose bags

A "humane fountain" in Detroit, ca. 1901–1906. (Library of Congress, LCCN 2016794663)

for horses. Walking down the street, you'd pass watering troughs and hitching rails. In 1900, there were 75,815 horses in New York City alone, a number that doesn't count the delivery ones who came in every day.[2] They pulled milk and laundry wagons, delivered groceries, and hauled enormous omnibuses. In the winter, sleigh horses wore bells so you could hear them coming on a snow-hushed street. Firefighters drove their horses three abreast, troika style, so they wouldn't tip over when they raced, top speed, to a fire.[3] Most horses worked different jobs over the course of their lives. Strong, young bus horses became hansom horses who might end their days pulling a peddler's cart.[4] Horse people of any era would recognize the smells of an equine-centered environment—manure, molasses, clover hay, neat's-foot oil—that wafted through the city. But the condition of the omnipresent horses, clip-clopping down every street, often escaped notice.

That was where humane agents came in. They turned up all over cities like New York, where they visited Madison Square Garden to check on

Fire horses in light harness in Washington, DC, ca. 1913. (Library of Congress, LCCN 2016853468)

Wotan, the circus horse who rose in a hot-air balloon accompanied by plenty of fireworks. His minder assured the committee that since the rider had to stay safe, the circus took care to preserve the horse's well-being.[5]

Humane societies' primary focus, however, was city workhorses, the often draft or draft cross "cyborgs," as historian Clay McShane has called them. They combined their power with those of men and machines to produce work. Worn-out streetcar drivers could sleep on the way back to the barn; the horses knew the way. Street railways encouraged teamsters to groom and name the horses they steered, since bonding would decrease cruelty and increase dedication. Plenty of the animals on the street were nourished, well tended, and able to perform the labor asked of them.

The dark side of all this equine work, however, was also visible. Horses died in the street, and sometimes urbanites saw painfully thin horses or lame ones, animals with goiters and wens, wheezing as they worked. They also watched drivers—some of whose jerky hands revealed scant experience with animals—overuse whips. The humane movement sought to address these wrongs.[6]

A woman feeds a horse while another person affixes a sun hat, 1907. (Library of Congress, LCCN 2005688915)

Women "in particular subscribed to the movement's ideology," writes Diane L. Beers in *For the Prevention of Cruelty*, "and demographically, they provided the backbone of animal advocacy."[7] Men presided—and handled the euthanizing—but women performed much of the day-to-day work of relief. With star-shaped badges on their coats, they scanned streetscapes for abused horses and testified on their behalf in court. They raised money for teamster education and summer-weight harnesses. They donated land for rest farms.[8] Women directed tag days, handing out metal bridle tokens to drivers of well-cared-for workhorses, or tagging those who looked hungry or ill-used.[9] The country's nascent Progressivism inspired a web between temperance and domestic abuse, animal cruelty and child neglect. New Women took part in this evolution. "Early female activists convincingly reasoned that protecting animals was crucial for the preservation of future families and future generations of children," writes Beers.[10]

People believed women's entreaties worked best, which both let men off the hook and forced women to the forefront. "Women can do more than men toward succoring abused horses," a humane official said in 1907. "When a man remonstrates with a brutal driver, unless he is an athlete the argument is likely to end disastrously for him when the driver gets down from his cart. But when a woman steps out from a crowd and speaks a word for a horse the driver must heed what she says, or else run away."[11] Here was the idealized image and sought-after result: the cruel teamster fleeing from a righteous woman and her metaphorical angel-fire sword.

The intersection of activists and workhorse relief was, however, complicated. Reformers "were not always people who knew horses and horse work well enough to distinguish between a working horse and an overworked horse," as Ann Norton Greene writes in her *Horses at Work*.[12] Many just disliked teamsters' yelling and thought of the laborers as coarse and brutish. When reformers emphasized horses' human qualities and handed out copies of Anna Sewell's *Black Beauty*, they "encouraged a sentimentalized image of horses as individuals of special sensitivity and intelligence," Greene writes. "They opened the door to the idea that having horses do any work, apart from pleasure riding and driving, was automatically a form of abuse."[13]

The first American edition of *Black Beauty* came out in 1890 and inspired works such as Mark Twain's 1903 anti-vivisection story *A Dog's Tale*. Activist and actor Minnie Maddern Fiske had asked Twain to write a book similarly depicting the plight of horses who become fodder in the bullfighting arena. In 1907, Twain published his anti-cruelty novella *A Horse's Tale*, like *Black Beauty* (partially) narrated by a horse. The story has a female protagonist, a young girl named Cathy, who lives on the Seventh Cavalry's army base along with Buffalo Bill Cody and his horse, her beloved Soldier Boy.[14] One night, she tumbles off Soldier Boy (coal black with a white star, just like Black Beauty), and he protects her from wolves. "People say a horse can't cry," he says, "but they don't know because we cry inside." The two become separated and don't reunite until Soldier Boy lies bleeding in Spain, gored in a bullfighting ring. Cathy rushes to him, and the bull attacks her too. Horse and girl die together, a grotesque revision of the joyful partnership between pairs like nineteenth-century novelist E. D. E. N. Southworth's young heroine Capitola Le Noir and her pony.

Twain's Cathy was an unusual activist not only because she was fictional and a child but because she wasn't an urban clubwoman who heeded the kind of sentiment in a 1905 *Baltimore Sun* editorial: "The Psalmist tells us that a horse is a vain thing to save a man. But it is certain that a woman is not a vain thing to save a horse, and in that work of salvation she should be aided and abetted by all good citizens."[15] Some, who appeared in the last chapter, occupied a place in urban society where they kept their own saddle horses or competed in shows. Others just liked animals and wanted to right societal ills. Protecting horses meant something, morally and spiritually, and led to various imaginative and focused drives, campaigns, and everyday behavioral shifts. Women were inclined to leave the inculcated dictates of "ladylike behavior" if it meant they were helping the voiceless. "Kindness is a religion," one Christian activist said, using faith appeals to encourage feminine kindness to animals. "Our Jewish sisters . . . will tell you that the Mosaic law teaches them kindness and care for the lower animals, while for us who follow the Christ, he has set up upon this humane work the seal of his benediction in the words, 'Blessed are the merciful.'"[16]

In 1896 New Orleans, the 159 women at an anti-cruelty meeting were, as a reporter wrote, "the best people of the community." Mrs. Florian Schaffter told the assemblage about "a sweet-voiced gentle woman" who'd helped get some laws passed. A branch of her organization, the Band of Mercy, formed in New Orleans. A horse there balked downtown one day. A bystander told the driver to hit the horse, and the driver refused. His daughter belonged to a Band of Mercy, he said, "and she asked me not to beat old Bob."[17] The Women's Branch of the Pennsylvania Society for the Prevention of Cruelty to Animals planned a night school to teach complex driving maneuvers—backing up, moving through tight spaces—without resorting to the whip.[18] And in Chicago, women, "well known in society and humane work," would walk along roads with horse-drawn vehicles, hunting unblanketed horses, or those with inappropriate shoes for ice and snow, and hang tags on their bridles. "To My Owner and Driver: Dear Master—Please blanket me, for I am cold. Feed, water, and shoe me regularly and see that my harness fits comfortably, for I can feel and suffer as well as yourself. I am speaking through the Anti-Cruelty society," read the tags.[19] Jessie Jordan, a humane officer in Texas, promoted a different kind of tag. Hers were tangible compliments, little medallions to hang from a bridle as a sign that the horse looked well, as a sort of gold star of approval.[20]

Humane associations didn't only take aim at working horse people. They also protested upper-class abuses such as docking, or surgical shortening, of

A mule-drawn streetcar, circa 1917. (Library of Congress)

horses' tails, which wavered in and out of fashion. Protesting docking could potentially offend people, including potential philanthropists or even family members, but activists persisted. Washington, DC, outlawed the practice, in which the tail muscle is severed and then cauterized, by 1897, but owners simply sent horses to nearby Virginia or Maryland.[21] Not only did docked horses endure pain, but they couldn't swat flies. Watching them try on a sweltering DC street was heartrending.[22] The SPCA asked that even the "smart set and upper ten" who rode with the Chevy Chase Hunt Club sign an anti-docking pledge. Once Theodore Roosevelt refused to buy or drive a horse with a maimed tail, the custom faded.[23] A bill was introduced before the Senate to make the practice illegal.[24]

Other fads included check or bearing reins, which held horses' heads high, creating an animated, prancing appearance but preventing them from pulling efficiently. (Many readers will remember that the bearing rein is a key theme in *Black Beauty*.) "Even women, who profess to be good and kind, complacently drive behind horses in the very throes of agony, due to tight check reins that stretch their mouths, strain their necks, expose their eyes to the sun's blinding rays and hold their heads so high, they are absolutely unable to see anything but the sky," wrote activist Anna Boyd in a Knoxville

58   ASTRIDE

newspaper in 1911. "Much suffering is unavoidable: but the aforesaid sickening variety is the result of cruelty deliberately inflicted, simply because the owners imagine it makes their horses look stylish and spirited."[25] Blinders, reformers argued, should at least be five inches from the eyes. "Go and feel of the tight blinders on any hard-working horse on a hot day and you will find those blinders damp, some of them soggy," one officer wrote.[26] Activists shamed their peers to effect change.

Everyday interactions with teamsters energized women activists. See something, say something could have been the humane societies' motto, and teamsters knew that any passerby could hail a society official to enforce regulations, derailing their day. Many anecdotes appeared in the press about women who intervened to help horses. A *Vogue* magazine columnist exhorted women readers to tell employers if they saw drivers drinking, a sort of turn-of-the-century version of the phone numbers printed on the back of trucks.[27] Women listened, and many reports surfaced of such interactions. In Chicago, in 1889, a horse fell on icy pavement. A nearby woman told the gathering group that she was a member of the anti-cruelty society, and that the horse just needed to be persuaded to get up. The horse didn't move when six people tugged on his bridle, so an ice salesman went to shove him with his boot. "No kicking," said the woman. She told people not to whip him or pull his tail. Finally, a group of men stood around him and lifted him. "I may have saved that poor, smooth-shod horse from a brutal beating," the woman said. "It was worth the time and the effort."[28]

To save horses, some women risked their lives, something newspapers reported. There was a fire in a nearby stable, one of New Yorker Mrs. Crashaw's servants told her one day in 1896. Mr. Crashaw used an alarm box to call the fire department, and when he ran to the stable, he saw his wife already pulling on the doors, which were indeed in flames. Fire galloped through the hayloft, too, while a group of men gaped from the alley. The Crashaws eventually managed to open the gates and saw the horses' terror. Mrs. Crashaw passed through all of that—fire overhead, straw on fire at her feet—threw her overcoat on top of the first horse and pulled him to safety. She did the same thing with the second horse, and when she emerged, firefighters had arrived.[29]

A Chicago woman blocked traffic on the busy Loop because she saw a horse so weak that he was bracing himself to stand. There was blood on his neck, presumably from being whipped. She hailed a police officer, who directed her toward an anti-cruelty society, but, as a crowd gathered, she insisted that the horse be unhitched and led to the police station. "That man will know better than to work a poor, suffering horse after this," she said.[30] In 1910, Dorothy Tronwig and three neighbors saw a coal and wood dealer drive his horses without watering them until they dropped. Tronwig and the others sponged down the exhausted horses and called the humane society. The dealer was brought up on charges.[31] In New York, a group of women surrounded a horse-car downtown because one of the horses looked sick. (He turned out to be suffering from a digestive ailment.)[32] Anti-cruelty society member Mrs. Anna Packard marched up to a teamster in Chicago in 1914 and asked if she could buy his horse. He said yes, for $35. She offered $2.50, and when he said no, she had him arrested for driving a crippled horse. She told the judge that she'd put the horse out to pasture at her society's farm.[33]

Chicagoan George Guy said he'd once cured an Indiana mule of balking by lighting some paper on fire and holding it underneath him, so when he saw a recalcitrant horse in the street one day in 1904, he showed the driver his method. An anti-cruelty society member named Mrs. L. W. Cady saw this procedure, called a police officer, and had Guy arrested. (As well as being inhumane, the fire/paper method didn't work.) She appeared in court, and he was fined twenty-five dollars. "This thing of being the 'Helpful Hints,' doesn't pay," Guy told a reporter. "Me, hereafter, the innocent bystander."[34]

In 1895, a reporter asked a New York woman who confronted a driver with four overladen horses if she was ever scared to confront an abusive teamster. "No," was the answer. "I think the men who treat their horses so badly are usually cowards and bullies. When they find you can use authority they are frightened and give in."[35]

In Topeka, Kansas, activists observed a plague of unfit horses, with maladies ranging from ringbones and spavins to poll evil (a swelling at the base of the head), fistula (another swelling, often at the withers), or contagious diseases. Activists alleged that horse traders gathered at the feed yards and traded hungry, thirsty, down-on-their-luck horses. Also, teamsters sometimes showed up with horses sored by ill-fitting harnesses. But as soon as teamsters heard humane officers were looking for them, they would just move the afflicted horses to another county or deny they owned them. Some even turned the horses out to wander the city.[36]

60   ASTRIDE

Other cities found that police officers did listen to women activists, articles said. In 1903, on Chicago's South Side, Ruth Ewing, Mrs. L. B. Root, and Mrs. Robert L. Gifford wore sheriff-style stars when stopping drivers of lame or victimized horses. Prosecutions went through the Illinois Humane Society. The women appeared as "complaining witnesses." Root estimated that she spent between one to three hours every day finding needy horses; one day, she found three within two hours. She wished more people would report cruelty but knew they were concerned about publicity. "These fears are groundless," she said. "When a case of cruelty comes to their notice it is only necessary to report it to the nearest policeman. He will secure the necessary evidence and make formal complaint against the offender. The person who calls attention to the abuse may be called upon to testify in court, but that is only a duty which is owing to the cause of humanity. No one should shirk such a duty."[37]

Reporters called the act of driving around looking for unfit horses "anti-cruelty slumming." One day, a group that had just opened a horse rest home in the suburbs gave journalists a tour. Driving the car was an anti-cruelty society officer, and a police officer rode along. Gifford would shout, "'There's a blinder,' or 'there's a lame one,' or 'there's a sore back,'" which, a reporter wrote, "acted like 'There she blows' upon a whaler." Activists would approach the horse's driver, show society-membership cards, and examine the horse, adjusting blinders that were too close to a horse's eye, for example. The group happened upon a scene with one police officer stopping a lame horse on the street's west side, another dealing with a needed blinder repair on the east. Amid this kerfuffle, a team of horses hit a cart and a horse landed against a trolley pole made of iron. "Mrs. Gifford jumped from the automobile and ran to the rescue of the injured horse," wrote a reporter. "Officers came to her assistance, and while that horse was being cared for the drivers of the two teams that had been stopped took advantage of the excitement to escape."[38]

Some fire stations left horses harnessed all day, except during their fifteen-minute grooming session, so the Chicago Commons Women's Club passed a resolution to request swinging harnesses, which hung above the horses, giving them a rest from their weight.[39] A letter to the editor in 1901 Washington outlined a local's distress at harsh bits, and a woman in Chicago demanded police officers help delivery horses whose legs cramped when they stood in knee-deep snowmelt.[40] On New Year's Eve 1913, anti-cruelty legions vowed to stop cab drivers who worked horses longer than twelve hours.[41] Activists monitored horse equipment, distributing fly nets, bitless bridles, chest protectors (to guard against tack that rubbed), summer bridles (lighter weight than some of the heavy harness), and chain shoes for better traction on macadam.[42] They exhibited confiscated bits and whips and railed against clipping horses, especially by poor owners who couldn't afford blankets.[43] For a while, women campaigned to have horses wear hats in the summer—bonnets, straw hats—for shade, but this faded when it became clear hats were too hot.[44] Humane society members in Mt. Vernon, NY, in 1904, requested guards posted by particularly steep hills as a deterrent to anyone inclined to whip a balker.[45]

In 1900, a convention of state societies preventing cruelty was scheduled to meet in Rochester, New York.[46] A statement about exactly what these societies wanted for horses—for example, more reporting of violent drivers— appeared in the *Chicago Daily Tribune* in January 1901. It complained that many tradespeople, like coal dealers and grocers, hired inexperienced drivers, who tended to whip horses more than seasoned horsemen did. "These poor animals are overdriven and then allowed to stand without blanketing, while the driver sits indoors chatting with the cook," the vividly rendered statement read. "At noon they are fed from bags so badly adjusted that half the grain falls to the street, and the empty, dusty, bags are left on to choke and smother the poor animals for the balance of the noon hour. They are badly shod in slippery weather and in winter their mouths are often blistered because the careless and ignorant driver inserts the bit without first taking the chill off by holding it against the animal's warm body."[47]

The Women's Auxiliary of the SPCA initiated workhorse parades in New York. Teamsters lined their horses up and proceeded past judges, who awarded prizes for displaying healthy horses. They sorted horses into "classes," depending on how many years they'd spent in the traces. Judges rated horses on their wind, soundness, and harness fit. Winners received cash, rosettes, and badges. The parade, with its ribbons and classes, was structured similarly to the shows that many of the SPCA's donors may have competed in or attended during the social season.[48]

At the seventh annual New York parade in 1913, about 2,500 horses marched by the reviewing stand, and a reporter recorded the names of police horses like Watercure, who led the procession. Next were fire horses,

A New York workhorse parade in 1909. (Library of Congress, LCCN 2014696727)

including Mormon, Madstone, and Robinhood. Workhorses included a thirty-seven-year-old called Joe and a thirty-six-year-old, Jim.[49] An announcement for one Chicago workhorse parade invited women to come meet the drivers who'd entered their horses and noted waggishly that animal lovers make good husbands.[50]

In the wintertime, humane associations sponsored Christmas trees and parties for horses. Women often staffed these seasonal events, at which drivers were urged to rest their horses during Christmas and give them apples and carrots. They served coffee and sometimes food to drivers, underlining the idea of humane treatment for all. The optics created a tableau of horses at rest, eating treats, aligning them with pets, worthy of attention, and kind treatment.[51]

Societies also sponsored drinking fountains for horses, some with multilevel drinking basins to accommodate dogs too. "These groups provided a link between temperance reformers and animal advocates, since fountain societies hoped that providing water would also encourage teamsters not to stop at saloons and thus reduce drunken abuse of horses," writes

Greene.[52] The New York Women's League for Animals sent a letter to the editor reminding readers of its water fountain in front of its Lafayette Street dispensary. Every hour during the summer, according to the league, around eighty horses drank. Signs reminded drivers to take the horses' bits out while watering.[53] Humane organizations funded and managed horse hospitals in various cities. In 1911, the New York Women's League planned to enlarge its animal hospital in the city, instead of the dispensary that was there in 1911.[54]

Hospitals, parades, Christmas parties. Should horses even be in the city? Not all the time, some activists thought. The New York Women's League for Animals had use in 1911 of a 250-acre farm upstate. A summer camp for boys used some of the land, and horses roamed the pastures. A rescue league also planned to give back about twelve formerly broken-down horses, "ready to go to work again as the bread-winners of the poor."[55] The Horse Aid Society maintained a sixty-five-acre rest farm near Ossining, New York. To send an overworked horse, explained the society's Mrs. Jacob Ehrlich, "All the man has to do is place his horse on board the ferryboat at the foot of Franklin Street, and it will be taken up to Ossining by the society and from there on to the farm." The ferry tender donated his services, and then horses and drivers walked the two and a half miles to the farm. Up to a hundred horses could be at the farm at a time and stay for a couple of weeks. The society would help drivers find temporary jobs while their horses rested. People endowed box stalls, so that horses with rich owners helped ones with poorer owners. One read, "In Memory of Bonny X," a racehorse, the ghost of the rich owner's horse hovering over the charity for the poor one.[56]

During World War I, Thoroughbred owners and breeders helped supply horses for the cavalry. Europeans had already bought up many American horses, first for the Boer wars, and then for their own wartime cavalries. Anita Baldwin, the daughter of racehorse owner Lucky Baldwin, believed that there could be a draft for horses. Following European custom, she started an American Red Star Animal Relief organization in America, a wartime humane association to serve army dogs and cavalry horses. "It is necessary that the Red Star be organized thoroughly in this country at the very outset of the war," she said. "This need is pointed out by the experience of the allies. Early in the European war thousands of animals were lost through lack of attention. Later, when

64   ASTRIDE

wounded animals were cared for, 150,000 out of 225,000 injured animals recovered, representing a value of $20,000,000 to the allies."[57]

For all the festive processions and straw hats, much of the humane work was preventing suffering by destroying sick or unwanted animals. Caring for animals always involves this unwelcome inevitability, and at the turn of the twentieth century, euthanasia played into the class tensions throughout the humane societies' dialectic. Being decent meant putting moribund horses down. There was a newspaper story about a man who bragged about selling a twenty-year-old lame horse. "Why, I'd have given you twice that amount to kill old Baldy kindly," the friend said, "and preserve a shred of my respect for you."[58]

The societies, as McShane notes, counted legally as "disinterested parties" when horses had to be killed. Owners found themselves bound to go along with SPCA plans for their animals.[59] If owners wanted insurance to pay for a dead horse, the horse had to be destroyed by a veterinarian or a humane official. "This regulation paradoxically led to the ASPCA, established to ensure the proper care of horses, becoming the primary horse killer in the city," writes Hilary J. Sweeney.[60] Women held an unusual position here. They advocated for merciful death—talking about it often and considering it the ultimate in animal stewardship—but didn't perform it themselves. In a time before horses were euthanized with injections, men shot suffering horses in the street. Guides for cavalrymen and humane officers alike showed, through diagrams, where a bullet should be aimed, and agents carried firearms for this purpose. Women could speak up for animals, but they couldn't shoot them.

Many urbanites endured the graphic sight of horses dying, according to journalistic coverage, sometimes through grisly accidents like the one that happened in 1900 when William Kelly was driving his employer's horse through New York City for some new shoes. The horse bolted and smashed into a truck. Terrified, he shook free of the driver and cart and kept running, crashing into another vehicle on busy Amsterdam Avenue where he was "almost disemboweled" by the wagon's pole. An SPCA agent shot him through the head.[61] In 1915, a Baltimore grocer's horse spooked and ran into a car. His injuries were terrible: two broken legs and a wound from a piece of car lodged in his side.[62] In 1905, a woman named Charlotte Loter, arms full of shopping packages, saw a broken-down and lame horse in New York, heaving in the shafts of a moving wagon. She approached the driver and told him the horse should be put down. "Oh, run along!" he said. Loter went to the police station and brought an officer to look at the horse. She wanted him shot. "You must be cold-blooded, ma'am," he said. Back at the station, Loter charged the man with cruelty to animals. The SPCA was notified, and an hour later, the horse was dead.[63]

These situations did not always end simply, and the humane societies did not always offer swift or graceful resolutions. In New York in 1909, a horse lay on a snowy street, and a passing horseman bought some laudanum and "sweet" (likely olive) oil and gave it to him because he thought he had colic. The driver asked him to call the SPCA, which he did. "He is not in very bad shape," the man told the SPCA, but the horse clearly did need some help. The driver put his wagon's tarp over the horse and rested his head on a burlap sack. Another onlooker asked if the SPCA had been called. Three other women walked by and asked the same thing. After almost three hours had passed, the original helper called again. The person on the phone said they'd dispatched an agent an hour ago; the society was very busy. By the time he got back to the horse, he'd been shot. "I don't know what I've done, boss, to have this come to me," the driver said. "This is the first job I've had in ten days. The animal society man has just been here and shot the horse." The original help-ing man found the agent drinking in a bar nearby and asked why he'd shot a horse who was in the middle of a mild colic attack. The agent wouldn't say.[64]

Some women worked outside the confines of humane organizations, helping, as they saw it, failing horses to die. Mrs. August Tommelin, in Chi-cago, purchased what she called "killers," or horses at the end of their lives. She did earn money, but said she wasn't motivated by that alone. Instead, she just loved horses so much that she was willing to have them put down.[65] She had gotten herself into this unusual position when she had rented her backyard at one point to a man who dealt with down-on-their-luck horses and realized that he made a good living. Tommelin bought neglected or starv-ing horses; she'd had twenty horses die in a month. She saw her strange job as a broker between horses and slaughterhouses as kind, since she was sav-ing them—with death—from fates worse than death. "A woman who loves horses cannot but be glad to have some of the poor creatures killed," she said.

> They suffer so, when ill or disabled, and some human beings are such utter brutes. Why, again and again I have interfered on behalf of ill or lame animals who were suffering abuse from their owners, and

Women at a Christmas celebration for horses, gathered around a tree, 1918. (Library of Congress, LCCN 2016869611)

I have reported such owners to the Humane society officers many times. I cannot bear to see the poor things suffer, and I see to it that they reach the end of their troubles gently. It would surprise many people to know how ignorant, unthinking and absolutely cruel many supposedly humane people are when it comes to working or disposing of a worthless horse.[66]

In her memoir, show horse rider Lida Fleitmann Bloodgood writes of buying an "ancient wreck" of a horse up for auction outside a horse show in Warrenton, Virginia. The horse's "bony manure-stained hips" were "raw and bleeding." She outbids several locals because, as she writes, the "old horse raised his hanging head and looked at me. I seemed to see, staring at me from his rheumy eyes, the tragedy of all old age, human or animal." She then takes the horse with her to go watch the races—the image is of her standing with a crowd of other highly accomplished, well-heeled riders, holding the old horse by a lead rope—but she must leave the next morning, so she takes him to the local hunt to be destroyed. "I myself led the poor old bag of bones to the Orange County kennels to be honorably fed to the hounds that, in younger days, he had perhaps galloped after," she writes.[67]

Today, humane activists focus on remaking slaughter-bound horses, turning ex-racehorses into riding horses, and fostering animals who can't be ridden, finding them homes as "pasture ornaments." In the New Woman's era, dedication toward equine rehabilitation mattered alongside providing a merciful death. This was unsurprising given that their society was horse-rich and that death—human and animal—more commonplace topics, as were lingering Victorian ideals. As Twain's Soldier Boy, the idealized horse, says, "To die—that does not disturb me; we of the service never care for death."

There were no horses inside the White City in the 1893 World Columbian Exposition, the Chicago event that was designed to emblematize the modern era. The clean, white streets were no place for manure, dirt, and animals. Following this trend, between 1910 and 1920, the number of urban horses in the United States halved, and it continued to diminish as cars took over city streets.[68]

The New Woman's enormous effort for and obsession with workhorses would peter out as the horses themselves left the urban landscape. But the legacy of this era remains in contemporary women's contribution to what we now know well as horse rescue, much of which focuses on Thoroughbred racehorse aftercare. As they do today, women in the late nineteenth and early twentieth centuries played important roles in Thoroughbred racing, from pedigree planning to breeding to riding and beyond.

4

Women in Racing

The era of the New Woman was also the golden age of American Thoroughbred racing. Boxing, baseball, and racing occupied the sporting imagination, and Americans held opinions on equine athletes like Man o' War, Exterminator, Sir Barton, and Morvich the way even today's most diffident observer still knows who's playing in the Super Bowl. Newspapers devoted entire sections to turf coverage. Big races made the front page.

Naturally, racing enthusiasts crossed over with other equestrian disciplines. The same families often owned racers as well as showing their own horses, foxhunting, and breeding. Women participated in many of these racing-adjacent activities. At the track, however, upper-class women mostly watched rather than took part, wearing formal clothes and the enduring elaborate hats. The great Exterminator was reputedly named by his owner's wife, as was Man o' War, but largely men trained, owned, rode, bred, and groomed racehorses.

Unlike horse show riders who entered themselves, the women who did make themselves part of racing often came in aslant, in novelty races, or away from the track itself. Elizabeth Daingerfield, a world-famous pedigree, breeding, and management expert, hardly ever went to the races. "I don't race them; I raise them," she said.[1] A gifted scholar of bloodlines, she managed a decade of Man o' War's stud years, creating a legacy of bloodlines that continues today. Daingerfield and a few Kentucky colleagues made large impacts on Thoroughbred racing, and others, like Oklahoman expert Eliza Carpenter, carved out widely varied places in their own worlds.

Mrs. R. T. Wilson and others attending a race at Saratoga. (Keeneland Library Cook Collection)

In 1878 California, two women, one in jockey silks, were seen riding astride in a city. Even something so minor caused people to wonder how it would work to have women in racing, as if it were the most absurd thing in the world. "The question now is," asked one writer, "will women in male attire be permitted to compete at the Fair for premiums offered for the best lady riders?"[2]

Josephine Clay may have been the first female Thoroughbred breeder, her great-grandson, Henry Clay Simpson, Jr., wrote in a biography. Her first husband, a grandson of statesman Henry Clay, died at the Battle of Vicksburg during the Civil War. She married his uncle John Clay, who owned a horse farm called Ashland.[3] Eleven Kentucky Derby winners trace lineage back to Ashland broodmares, and Clay also bred a horse named Kentucky, a son of the famous Lexington, the stallion at the center of Geraldine Brooks's 2022 novel *Horse*.[4]

When John Clay traveled with racehorses, Josephine, along with a formerly enslaved horseman named Harve, stayed at home to manage the farm. The Clays took part in private races held at Ashland's track, and owned a famous broodmare named Skedaddle.[5] Cavalry commander George Armstrong Custer bought one of their racers, Victory. John Clay died in 1887, and Clay became recognized as a pioneer horsewoman. Riley, a colt she bred, won the 1890 Kentucky Derby with celebrity jockey Isaac Murphy aboard.[6] As a woman, she couldn't join the Jockey Club, but she would go to the Phoenix Hotel in downtown Lexington to play poker with other managers.

Clay also wrote fiction. One short story, "Who Rode La Sylphide," features a young, newly married woman. "'Don't be shocked,'" she tells her husband, "'but once upon a time I was a terrible tomboy.'" Her past, she says, involved plenty of riding. "I took to horses, and horses took to me—I have broken many a colt no one else could do anything with."[7] Later in the story, a mysterious jockey, identity obscured by a scarf, appears just in time to ride a crucial race. Although the jockey is hustled off, he eventually appears to be the owner's "terrible tomboy" wife, posing as a boy. This may have been based on reality, Simpson writes, as Clay had "told her grandchildren that she had ridden and won a private match race for her husband."[8] Clay died in 1920, and her will specified that Ashland would be entailed during her daughters' lives.[9]

Like Clay, Elizabeth Daingerfield managed Thoroughbred farms. And people found that you hadn't come about horses, you'd have to work hard to find her. One rainy morning in 1922, a reporter located Daingerfield in an outbuilding, wearing her usual uniform of work boots, an old skirt, and a faded black sweater. Daingerfield gave orders, inspected pastures, scratched dogs' ears, and checked every horse on the place before inviting the reporter to sit down. When the two finally had the chance to talk—they sat smoking together after a Kentucky ham-and-biscuits lunch—the reporter had to ask: how did Daingerfield keep going, day in and day out?

"With humans you now and then think, 'Oh, what's the use to believe or to disbelieve in them?'" Daingerfield said, in her husky voice.[10] "But with fine horses there's always a never-ending inspiration to believe."[11]

At the track, jockeys around the turn of the century were chiefly white men. The celebrity Black jockeys of the Reconstruction era and late nineteenth century had been run off by racist policies. Women generally did not race horses against men, but there were some notable exceptions.[12]

Scattershot mentions of women entering racing peppered the contemporary press. Brief profiles, sometimes in women's sections, sports sections, or local news, demonstrated that these racing women constituted news in a way that horse show competitors did not. Many of the mentions are brief, as if the fact that the women existed was enough to merit being written up. In 1889, a mention appeared in the *Sacramento Bee* about the "only female jockey in the world" (an appellation she'd share with many others name-dropped in articles). Her name was Mattie Dyson. She wore black and red jockey silks, she was twelve years old, and her father raised racehorses.[13] Around the same time, there was a female jockey riding on the Pacific coast circuit identified only as Mrs. Bagwill—another "only woman jockey"—who wore standard jockey clothes and won two of five races at the Nevada State Fair.[14] She wore divided skirts, astride, and rode forward, as men jockeys did.[15]

Ada Evans Dean entered her Thoroughbreds Moorish Prince and Moorish Dance in county-level races in 1905, then went home while their trainer settled them in at the fairgrounds. Next, he sent a telegram that said, "Come at once. [Jockey] McNamara cannot ride Moorish Prince." She'd ride him herself, she decided, and dressed in her own silks. The judges said no for a long time but finally conceded. Thousands watched her not only race but win.[16]

In this period, Americans also avidly followed harness racing, in which jockeys drive horses rather than ride them. Some women participated glancingly in this sport as well as flat or Thoroughbred racing. Hoosier Cora Pontifax broke her own colts and won the gentlemen's driving class at a county fair with her horse Tucker, where a crowd turned out to watch "the strange spectacle of a woman driving."[17] Mary B. Crosby drove her mare Emma B. at the New Hampshire Trotting-Horse Breeders' Association meeting in 1894. Crosby wore red and cared for her horses as well as trained them. "Some of the people thought it was a terrible thing for a woman to do," she said. Her husband, however, supported her, and she became the most popular driver at the track. She was as much at home in the sulky as in her parlor, she said.[18] The wife—notably unnamed given that the article featured her—of a Connecticut trainer named "Knap" McCarthy drove her mare, Annie Mace, on the Speedway. She also cared for Knap's charges and worked them when he was away. She drove about fifty miles a day, keeping the trotters in shape. "Few trainers can jog and care for their horses with more skill," a reporter wrote.[19]

Kate Caton, a Lansing, Michigan woman, bought and trained her own trotters. Her eighty-acre farm included a racetrack. "She talks in short, quick sentences," said an 1896 article, "and what she says is businesslike and decisive. She asks no advice, and never hesitates." The reporter also wanted to hear her opinions on her role-defying occupations, but Caton wasn't interested. "She is too busy to talk about the new woman, and the emancipation of her sex," the reporter wrote.[20]

Early in the twentieth century, Dorothy Kincel made headlines as a jockey. Depending upon the account, she was either twelve or fourteen years old. Reputedly born in the eastern part of the country, Kincel was said to have been raised on a western ranch. Kincel spoke, however, with the wisdom and assurance of a much older rider. "The horse is not to blame," she said. "It's bad treatment that makes him ugly and fear of him that makes a poor rider."

People said Kincel had big hands, strong shoulders, and could lift a hundred pounds, but photographs from a magazine show her as the child she was. She posed with her trick horse, a big-bodied chestnut with a blaze who carries a whip in his mouth. A South Dakota wind blows his tail and the girl's skirts, and Kincel looks off toward a horizon with a cap pulled down, shading her eyes. In another photograph, she is atop her horse, leaning forward, jockey-style, with her tall boots showing underneath a short riding skirt.[21] A third shows Kincel from behind, waiting with a group of male jockeys for an exercise session to start. You can see the ribbons in her pigtails, tied back as she readies to gallop. "She has established a reputation as a girl jockey in Montana, the two Dakotas, Minnesota, Iowa and other western states, and has met with very considerable success when riding against boy jockeys," the caption ran. "She trains her own horses, and is, to some extent at all events, her own stable-boy."[22] To be exceptional didn't only mean winning races and keeping up with far more experienced jockeys. It also meant—with the emphasis on the gender—being her own boy.

Like male jockeys, Kincel rode under contract, racing in fair circuits. She traveled with her mother, once sleeping in a freight car in her sweaty jockey clothes because there were too many drunk men in the other cars. As fierce and independent as Kincel seemed, she also understood the limitations her

A 1913 novelty race against time featuring Madame Marantette driving an ostrich harnessed with a horse. (St. Joseph County Historical Society of Michigan)

circumstances presented. There would be no life as a wage-earning rider in Kentucky or Maryland. "She says she would dearly love to ride a really good horse in a big race," an article said, "but she sees no prospect of getting out of South Dakota."[23]

Some tracks or fairs hosted women's "novelty races," which often earned mentions in the press. One horse got so excited during one of these that he ran off a high bank into the river with his rider, solely named as Mrs. Bowers, still aboard. The crowd stared, watching as Bowers tried to turn him away from the bank, but it was useless; she just readied herself. Everyone on horseback raced toward the river. Bowers stuck tight, swam her horse out of the river, and rode back, smiling, to the "wild applause of the spectators."[24]

At a similar novelty race at the Bergen County Fair, a jockey named Madge Clarke might have won the quarter-mile dash if she hadn't had to hang on to her hat.[25] A North Carolinian steeplechase jockey was listed as the only woman jockey in another race that day. She was thrown but not hurt.[26] At a women's race in 1920 at a Maryland fair, a stretch duel in the drizzle carried the crowd to its feet. "These young ladies proved themselves capable horsewomen," a reporter wrote, "and when it came to a whipping finish both knew how to apply the baton."[27] Girl jockeys raced at Columbia Park in Buffalo, sponsored by the Hygienic Club, which had more to do with health, a nod to the goddess Hygeia, than cleanliness. One of the heats was won in fifty seconds, described as a world record for women's races. The locals at least believed they'd seen history.[28]

By 1918, many American male jockeys were away fighting in World War I. Barbara Barnes, riding races in Chadron, Nebraska, was listed as "one of the few ladies who now holds such a position."[29] Rose Mallaly, described as a "professional woman jockey," collided with another female rider at Stockton, California one day, and horses and riders all went down around the same time that rider Margaret Leigh inherited the "only woman jockey in America" appellation.[30] In 1922, Lorena Trickey, an Oregon rider who had been a jockey on the local circuit, came to New York and applied for her license, claiming that she won all the prizes she could as a cowgirl. She wanted to earn more money on the eastern turf.[31]

Hollywood made a movie about a fictional girl jockey named Mickey, a cross between a circus-foundling story and a Kincel-type profile. "Mickey" traces a "harem-scarem tomboy" from her daredevil origins to the day she plans to topple an intricate plot by posing as a jockey and riding in a horse race. In a moment recalling Josephine Clay's ride and foreshadowing *National Velvet's* gender subterfuge, Mickey falls from a horse, revealing when her hair spills from her helmet that she's a girl.[32]

Elizabeth Daingerfield's father, Foxhall Daingerfield, practiced law. He studied and loved horses, and always kept at least one broodmare on the family farm.[33] There were five girls and three boys.[34] Elizabeth, born in 1870, was the second-eldest daughter, and she and her brother Algernon inherited their father's obsession, riding the countryside.[35] Algernon remembered the day he found his sister inside a stallion's paddock, feeding the horse apples one after another. Not wanting to alarm the stallion, Algernon whispered to his sister that he wanted to tell her something. Slowly, Elizabeth walked over to her brother, the stallion trailing, gnawing the apples she held over her shoulder as they walked.[36]

Foxhall Daingerfield brewed his own liniment and taught his children all he knew about horses. No firing irons, he said. Keep pastures big so horses can move around naturally.[37] If two mares fight, pasture them together and they'll become friends.[38] To know if a horse will win, ask his dam.[39] "Greatness in a horse may be an accident," Foxhall Daingerfield said, "but stick to the families that have the greatest number of accidents."[40] Elizabeth internalized the lessons, notated bloodlines in her own pedigree book, and wrote down his liniment recipes. In the 1870s, when Sanders Bruce began compiling American bloodlines into the American Stud Book for 1873, he relied upon Foxhall Daingerfield's knowledge.[41] So did his brother-in-law, financier James Keene, who'd decided to start a racing stable in 1879.[42] In 1892, Daingerfield's health deteriorated, and the house in Harrisonburg burned down. Daingerfield moved his family to Lexington, Kentucky to run Keene's new stud farm, Castleton. There, Daingerfield put into practice the theories he had honed on his Virginia bloodstock farm. Elizabeth, twenty-two years old, worked alongside her father.

Daingerfield's theories worked. By 1907, the aggregate winnings of Castleton horses were $397,342, meaning that Keene had won more money in one year than any other turfman ever.[43] Castleton horses included the megastars of the era. Colin, Sysonby, Ballot, Peter Pan, and Delhi had all won more than $100,000 under the blue-and-white polka dot silks.[44] Foxhall Daingerfield's pet project was the stallion Ultimus, a son of Commando, a chestnut who seemed bigger than he was.[45] His name came from his position as the culmination of years of breeding. "My ideal sire must have speed and courage," Elizabeth Daingerfield would say, years later. "He mustn't be too big—16 hands at the most. He must be muscular. You have seen Ultimus. He is my type to perfection."[46]

By about 1909, Foxhall Daingerfield was sick, and traveling back and forth to Baltimore for electrical absorption treatment. His daughter had become the practical manager of the farm.[47] She saw every animal every day when she was home, she said. "And I am seldom away from home."[48] In 1912, with both her father and uncle seriously ill, Castleton had to be sold. His children were at Foxhall Daingerfield's bedside when he died, all except Elizabeth's brother Algernon. He was in New York arranging his uncle's funeral. James Keene had died on January 3, 1913, and Foxhall Daingerfield followed on January 5, never knowing Keene was gone.[49]

After Daingerfield's father died, most of the horses went to nearby Kingston Farm. Daingerfield worked with the horses and patented her father's liniment, brewing it in a laboratory space and selling it through the mail.[50] In April, a barn caught fire. Two mares kicked down a door and escaped with

Elizabeth Daingerfield. (Keeneland Library Cook Collection)

their foals. Daingerfield raced toward the barn at the head of the rescue party, but by the time she got there, fifteen horses had burned to death. Police suspected arson, but their bloodhounds couldn't find a trail, and Daingerfield grieved openly.[51]

In September, the Castleton horses traveled by train to Madison Square Garden in New York City for an enormous dispersal. It was a huge, heartbreaking event. Famous auctioneer George Bain described the horses one by one. More than three thousand people watched and understood what was for sale: the living, breathing results of an extraordinary partnership. Daingerfield, standing by, saw each led to the auction block. Then, an unlikely savior appeared. A Cleveland iron millionaire named Price McKinney bought twenty-six of the horses, including Colin and Ultimus.[52] Colin went for $39,000 or close to a million dollars today. McKinney had never owned racehorses before, but Kentuckians happily learned he planned to return them to Kingston Stud, with Daingerfield managing.[53] She telegrammed the farm staff to ready the stalls.

The image of Daingerfield and Colin on the cover of the September 20, 1913, *Thoroughbred Record*—which seems to be a pastiche of two photographs—commemorates the moment. In it, Daingerfield stands in the foreground, her long skirt and fitted jacket reminiscent of a sidesaddle habit. She wears a dark, brimmed hat, and looks toward Colin, who in turn stands grandly, a ringed snaffle in his mouth and his tail slightly held aloft.

The horses, now co-owned by McKinney's partner, Corrigan, stabled at Kingston and under Daingerfield's care, became known as Wickliffe Stud.[54] McKinney expanded the land by leasing 250 adjoining acres, making the total around 700.[55] The paddocks, as Daingerfield had been taught, were spacious.[56] When Daingerfield's colts arrived at Gravesend in New York for training that spring, horsemen saw well-conformed, adaptable animals.[57]

Around 1921, Daingerfield began speaking out on a favorite topic: her opposition to racing two-year-olds. (Her champion Luke McLuke, who didn't race at two, would become an example of how well this worked.)[58] She trained young horses on turf instead of hard dirt and said the popular practice of handicapping (where certain racers carry lead bars in their saddle pads) forced horses to bear too much weight.[59] She referred to racing two-year-olds as "the slaughter of the innocents" and wrote that "if the racing interests were interested in breeding instead of in betting, we should have a standard of thoroughbreds such as we can only dream about now."[60] Daingerfield also wrote book reviews and instructional articles. One piece advocated for roomy stalls. "One does not buy diamonds and keep them in a coal scuttle," she wrote. "Why give approximately as much for a horse and keep him in a woodshed?"[61]

She gave advice, both in writing and through interviews. Don't breed horses with ringbone. Don't depend on yearling sales for your horses; better to run your own farm. Don't try to make up for poor feeding with quickly acquired "soft flesh" for the sales ring.[62] Her horses were good-tempered, she said, because she allowed no harsh treatment.[63] Noise around a horse was dangerous, and a man who carried a club into a stable would probably get killed one day and, frankly, he should. "The big thought about taking care of horses is to love them, to care about them," she said.[64] Her assistant, John Buckner, shared Daingerfield's passion for detail and obsessive memory. He once fired a groom for being loud.[65] "Some men are alike as peas," she told a reporter, "but I never knew two well bred horses to be alike. They are individual, sincere, and courageous. A horse never lies to you."[66]

By 1917, America had entered World War I. Corrigan, who had bought McKinley out the year before, decided to disperse Wickliffe. Instead of

Daingerfield in later years. (Keeneland Library Cook Collection)

Madison Square Garden, the sale took place in January 1918, in Lexington. A storm roared on sale day.[67] The sky hurled ice, snow, and rain. Snowdrifts forced Kingston's gates closed, so a neighbor tore down his fencing so that all the guests could enter.[68] Horsemen filed into the stables. They peered in stalls and gathered, in hats and overcoats, under a big tent for hot bowls of burgoo and to say goodbye.[69] Daingerfield had sold everything she could to raise money, hoping to keep Ultimus.

"What am I offered for Ultimus?" the auctioneer asked.

"Every cent I have in the world, $20,000," she said.

That wasn't enough. This time, no McKinney heroics saved the day. Ultimus, now fifteen, sold for $26,000.[70]

Next, Daingerfield tended a modest nursery at a farm called Haylands, where she lived with her sisters. She sent a scant four yearlings at the Saratoga sale. She had returned to a beginning, a dauntless response to a cycle of loss and rebuilding. Horsemen approved of the handsome youngsters Daingerfield raised. But without Ultimus, her way forward was less certain.[71]

In 1920, the great chestnut Man o' War broke records, grabbed headlines, and reigned as the undisputed king of Thoroughbred racing. He was the most famous horse in the world, the Horse of the Century. Voluble and flush with success, his owner Sam Riddle could have hired anyone to take care of Man o' War's transition from racehorse to stud. He chose Daingerfield.

Film whirred in cameras and two thousand people pressed against the rail the day Man o' War made his last public appearance, galloping up and back at the Lexington racetrack, soggy with just-melted snow. The master of ceremonies announced, to cheers, that the horse would be in the care of "the premier horsewoman of America."[72]

"He's a vigorous, healthy horse," Daingerfield said. "Seems to have a fine disposition. We shall be friends."[73] When a reporter pointed out what a coincidence it was that Man o' War, who never raced there, would wind up in Kentucky, she said, "A coincidence, perhaps, that he should return to Kentucky, but not a coincidence that he should be born here. Kentucky is the only place on earth where the perfect horse could have been born."[74]

Trainer and jockey Eliza Carpenter did not enjoy the same privileged background as Daingerfield but shared her passion and expertise. Carpenter was born enslaved in Virginia and sold at six years old to an enslaver in Kentucky, and then again to one in Missouri. She didn't remember exactly when, she said. "I can't figure it up, but I was put on the block and sold as an eight-year-old the fall before the Civil War broke out in the spring."[75]

After emancipation in 1865, Carpenter returned to Kentucky, where she fell in love with Thoroughbred horses. With talent and skill, she decided to make horses her life. Next, she moved to Kansas and became a trainer. Later, she made the land run into Oklahoma along with other Sooners. She staked a claim and continued to train racehorses. She raced her own stable as far as Tijuana, and trained horses called Jimmy Rain, Sam Carpenter, and Irish Maid. If she didn't like a jockey's performance, she'd simply ride her own horse.[76]

In 1887, a newspaper reported that Carpenter had "taken her fast horses to Winfield [Kansas]." She went to fairs in Independence, Kansas, and entered one horse, named Maud S., in a walk-trot-running race.[77] Once, she mounted a chestnut mare and tried for a thousand-dollar prize offered to the first person who could get to the Ponca City side of the Cherokee Strip. She urged the mare on and made it faster than the first train but lost.[78] When others had started shipping racehorses by trail, Carpenter still traveled with in a wagon outfitted for camping and a dog along for the journey.[79]

She suffered some bad luck. In 1894, Carpenter reported three lost horses: a brown horse with a wart, a swaybacked light bay mare, and a bay mare with four white feet and a branded C on its left shoulder.[80] One night in 1897, she left a horse to graze near a canal. He was gone in the morning, and she and police officers were sure he'd been stolen. There were men's footsteps nearby.[81] One of Carpenter's horses, a likely four-year-old worth $250, died when a threshing machine went by his stable yard, and he tried to run through the fence.[82]

On a clear, cool Sunday in September 1906, Carpenter rode in the 101 Ranch's Wild West Show, recreating the Oklahoma land rush. Fifty thousand people came to the show; the Santa Fe railroad had added twenty trains. Keeping the peace at the performance—there was no liquor allowed—were police officers and some National Guardsmen. Tribes who took part in the two-thousand-person parade leading up to the performances included Pones, Otoe, Osage, Kaw, Pawnee, Cheyenne, Arapahoe, Apache, Sioux, and Tonkawa.

There were two thousand performers in the program. A steer did get loose and threatened to run into the crowd, but a cowboy caught him. Somehow, the only injury was to a cowboy's knee when a pony fell on him. Audiences watched a cowboy rope and kill a buffalo, later served in sandwiches.[83] The show also featured bronco busting, a cowgirl quadrille, and Bill Pickett, the legendary Black cowboy who invented bulldogging, in which cowboys chase a steer at speed, go from horse to steer, and wrestle the steer down.[84]

Carpenter, standing up in her buggy "like a Roman charioteer," took the first claim and first prize in the competition surrounding the reenactment of the land rush.[85] In the actual race, thirteen years prior, Carpenter had ridden astride, covering twelve miles in forty-five minutes. This was a time to recreate that accomplishment in public and with her famously fast racehorses.[86]

Carpenter died at home in Ponca City from a fractured skull after a buggy accident, a fearless horsewoman to the last, and a pioneer in a time that white owners dominated both large and small-scale horse racing. An obituary listed her as one of the only Black racing stable owners in Oklahoma, one of the few in the West, and "for many years one of the best known [to] racing followers."[87]

In 1923, Man o' War's owner and Daingerfield's employer, Sam Riddle, bought a farm in a partnership with his niece's husband Walter Jeffords. They

Cornelia Averell Harriman Gerry, Ral Parr, a patrol judge, and Mrs. Frank Bishop at Saratoga. (Keeneland Library Cook Collection)

called the new place Faraway Farm. (Local papers, however, called it "Miss Daingerfield's Faraway Farm.")[88] There, she cared for other famous horses including Morvich, American Flag, Mars, and Golden Broom.[89]

Man o' War's twenty-by-twenty box stall was a foot deep in straw, and he ate mixed bran and oats from special safety feed tubs, made by a Lexington tinsmith. He drank water from a farm spring. Insurance company regulations said Man o' War was never to be out of sight, so Buckner or a groom watched over him all the time.[90] Daingerfield shuttled between three farms in her charge: Haylands, Faraway, and Elmendorf. She ran to long-distance phone calls, handled the crush of visitors to Man o' War, and stayed up nights with sick animals. Haylands alone housed over thirty dogs, Daingerfield's purebred English sheepdogs and collies as well as strays. There were cats, goats, and, briefly, a brown bear that wound up at the Cincinnati Zoo.[91] She particularly adored Morvich, the 1922 Kentucky Derby winner, who stood at Haylands,

John Buckner and Man o' War. (Keeneland Library Jeffords Collection)

partially because his grand-dam, Running Stream, had been her favorite mare back in her father's day.[92]

Man o' War proved such an attraction that Lexingtonians knew to give the same directions as soon as a newcomer rolled down the car window. Go under the railroad bridge, go about three and a half miles, and turn into the Riddle Farm.[93]

Daingerfield and Buckner showed the horse to Japanese missionaries, nurses' conventions, and, on an average Sunday, a thousand fans. He became racing's greatest ambassador.[94] Two boys ran away from home to see him, and when the probation officer brought them to the farm, Daingerfield let the youngest hug the stallion and gave them two pigs to take back to Indiana.[95] Was Man o' War the greatest racer? a reporter asked once. "What horse would you name before him?" she asked tartly.[96]

Daingerfield's stature grew. Through the *New York Telegraph*, she held a naming contest for a colt she bred by Under Fire and Temptation. The name

Steadfast, entered by four different people, won.[97] And while Man o' War was her most famous client, Daingerfield advised many, many more clients about breeding. She traveled to England to choose mares and advised James Brady to buy Tea Biscuit—who went on to be the dam of Hard Tack, Seabiscuit's sire—from Arthur Hancock.[98]

Daingerfield's sex rarely escaped mention. Like Gerken, the show rider and show horse breeder, she wasn't "distressingly masculine," one reporter reassured readers. Daingerfield became the first woman to breed a Futurity winner, Ultimus's filly Step Lightly, in 1920.[99]

She retired on October 11, 1930, after taking care of Man o' War for ten years. This was "on the best of terms," as she said, "and deeply regret that circumstances necessitate my separation from Man o' War, which I consider the greatest horse of all time."[100] Daingerfield continued to manage Haylands and her own horses as well as do her breeding consultation work. She visited New York, guesting on sportswriter Grantland Rice's radio show.[101] She wrote in the *Blood-Horse* that yes, there were too many undesirable Thoroughbreds. But instead of spaying mares or limiting breeding—instead of blaming the horses—she wanted to get rid of shoddy horse people. "It is the elimination of the horse-owner who is neither horseman nor sportsman that we need," she wrote.[102]

In 1939, Daingerfield traveled to California for the premier of the movie *Kentucky*, which starred Norma Shearer and Walter Brennan. She attended at movie executives' homes and made a trip to Agua Caliente and a visit to the set of *The Wizard of Oz*. She loved the smell of eucalyptus wood, she said, and rode through San Francisco with the fire chief there. And she enjoyed the sight of Castleton and Walnut Hall on film, although she couldn't help noticing that the Kentucky Derby scene wasn't one race but was patched together from five. She praised her traveling companion, Kentucky Governor "Happy" Chandler, because he managed to demonstrate "how a sweet country boy can be a great cavalier in the modern world of movie make-believe."[103]

Daingerfield lived with her sisters at Haylands until they died, and then she moved to a care facility. She died on her eighty-first birthday.[104]

Daingerfield was not the only woman manager in the Thoroughbred industry. In 1923, the governing board of the Southern California Jockey Club elected as head racehorse owner and Kentuckian Caroline Schreiber. "Because of her thorough knowledge in all matters pertaining to the equine kingdom, Miss

The Belmont gates, 1905. (Keeneland Library Cook Collection)

Schreiber has been chosen for the honor of being America's first race track queen in fact as well as action," the club announced.[105] And back in Kentucky, Daysie Proctor worked as the secretary of Hamburg Farm. Both she and Daingerfield were on the horse show committee at the Blue Grass Fair. (Through the 1930s, Proctor would go on to remain a key figure in Lexington and Thoroughbred racing.)

In a piece for a series called "Women Who Lead the Way," a reporter positioned Daingerfield as the only woman who managed a Thoroughbred farm, with "perhaps one exception," probably an allusion to Elizabeth Kane, who was similar in stature to Daingerfield. Kane managed financier August Belmont's farm, Nursery Stud. "The feminist invasion has overrun the thorobred [sic] racehorse field," wrote reporter Robert Dundon in 1921. "If you don't believe it pay a visit to Lexington and you will soon discover that the two principal nurseries of equine supremacy are in solo charge of the gentler sex."[106] Both were listed as having "high class foals" in a 1918 story, and Kane was featured in a syndicated "About Women" column as "one of the best known breeders of race horses in the world."[107]

Man o' War as a young horse. (Keeneland Library Cook Collection)

In 1925, Kane ran a dispersal sale. "It is notable, by the way, that the forthcoming sale . . . will also find the horses brought to the ring by a woman; Mrs. Elizabeth Kane, who has managed Nursery Stud since the death of her husband," said an article.[108] When Adolphe Pons, who had been Belmont's secretary for twenty-four years, took over the lease on Nursery Stud, journalists took pains to mention that he would "continue the breeding of thorobred [sic] horses there under the management of Mrs. Elizabeth Kane," a partnership that would continue for many years.[109]

There were plenty of mentions of both women, who helped each other out. One night, Daingerfield was overseeing a birth when the mare died. Kane immediately sent a nurse mare to save the baby.[110]

For all the bloodline study and the tangible impact their work made on today's Thoroughbreds, women like Kane and Daingerfield understood the ineffable. Others—jockeys, trainers, breeders—shared their devotion to racing, even as it remained largely a space designated for men.

One day in 1929, Daingerfield stood at Man o' War's paddock with a reporter. The two of them watched the stallion in the early spring sunshine, the light wind ruffling his mane, and the man wondered what made this one horse so different from all the others. "Heart," Daingerfield told him. "An unbeatable heart."[111]

Understanding a horse's personality and spirit—his heart—was something that cowgirls experienced in a way trainers like Carpenter and Daingerfield would have understood. From ranchers to spangled performers, cowgirls took horse culture from curated and pedigreed to something that was wild and made for show.

5

Cowgirls

In 1888, a man riding through Oregon heard a thunderous footfall behind him. First came some young horses, racing downhill. Alongside them pounded a rider on a horse who threw off wet foam. "We stared in a way that was not mannerly, even in the wilds of Oregon," wrote the man. "The rider of the restless pony was a young girl."[1]

Another story, this one from New Mexico, said that cattlemen kept spotting a beautiful woman riding a spirited bay horse. But none of them could catch up with her. They called her "the ghost woman," and in their scarcely populated area, her identity mystified locals. One man saw her drink from a stream but then vanish. A trio of others saw her sitting still on her horse, her hair blowing in the wind. As soon as they approached, she touched her horse with a spur and galloped off. "I don't know what to make of it," one of the cowpunchers said. "How she got away I don't know."[2]

Originally, cowgirls were confusing. They seemed the cowboy's natural other half, but their western newness also made them modern, powerful women of a kind not seen before, melding manual laborers and Amazonian horsewomen. "The cowboy was born in Mexico, but women homesteaders were among the first cowgirls: a new, truly American persona that symbolized western women's can-do agency and independence and soon fascinated the nation," writes Winifred Gallagher.[3] "A genuine female cowboy" was reported in 1893, when the term "cowgirl" still wasn't in common usage.[4]

Many women needed to ride in the West. Native women, like the famous Apache warrior Lozen, fought alongside military leaders, including

A girl herding her family's cattle in Lawton, Oklahoma, in 1917. (Library of Congress, LCCN 2018678183)

Geronimo.[5] Women homesteaders and ranchers rode astride and hunted for game. Part of the mythology surrounding the entertainer-cowgirl stemmed from her origin story as a daring, natural rider who performed horseback chores like riding fences, moving cattle, and homing herds.

Over time, the term "cowgirl" mutated from meaning a woman solely doing what was necessary for a pioneer life to more of a performer. What started at home continued in shows like Buffalo Bill's Wild West as a sight for urban and eastern audiences, who thrilled to see tasks learned on the range—roping, shooting, and riding—taken to showy levels. Cowgirls ignited American imagination, and even today, the cowgirl and female rodeo rider of the early twentieth century are some of the best-chronicled horsewomen of the era. "Based on these historical realities and the diversity of cowgirl experiences, twentieth- and twenty-first century historians have made a careful delineation between cattle women and rodeo entertainers. . . . Yet, from the 1900s through the 1920s . . . performers sold audiences on the notion that rodeo cowgirls were the daughters of true pioneer mothers with ranching in their blood," writes Rebecca Scofield in her study *Outriders*.[6]

This photograph, "Texas Rider," was likely taken in Utah or Colorado. (Library of Congress, LCCN 2006679874)

Wild West shows first took hold in the 1880s, and the most famous, including Buffalo Bill's Wild West, the 101 Ranch Wild West Show, and Pawnee Bill's Wild West, showcased cowgirls. They ran races, did rope tricks, and put trick horses through their paces. Additionally, the Calgary Stampede of 1912 highlighted cowgirls competing against men and expanded the reach of famous performers such as Lucille Mulhall, Bertha Blancett, and Fannie Sperry Steele.[7] Audiences loved to look at them. Many cowgirls performed at Oregon's Pendleton Round-Up, a frontier-day celebration.[8] One of these, Mulhall, is often called the first cowgirl. She stands as a key example of a western woman who went from ranch work to performing success. Even if she was not the "first cowgirl," a hard superlative to prove, the cowgirl, in Mulhall's presentation, was a sight to behold.

Some credit sharpshooter Annie Oakley with creating the cowgirl's dual identity of living a horse-focused, athletic life while remaining conventionally feminine. As Glenda Riley writes, Oakley hewed to Victorian ideas of

Wild West show star Calamity Jane, 1901. (Library of Congress, LCCN 2005688173)

propriety even while cowgirl performances placed her firmly (along with Calamity Jane) in the transgressive camp. A household name to this day, Oakley grew up in Ohio. Her story inspired the musical *Annie Get Your Gun*, which debuted on Broadway in 1946. Born Phoebe Ann Moses, Oakley learned her skills hunting for game. She went on the road with her husband, Frank Butler, whom she'd bested in a shooting contest. She did all her riding stunts sidesaddle, in a long skirt, shooting while her horse galloped around the arena. She trained horses to do tricks. One, Gypsy, climbed stairs and entered an elevator.[9]

The cowgirl inhabited the real West as well as the mythological Wild West during a time when, as historian Frederick Jackson Turner told an audience at the 1893 World Columbian Exposition, the frontier was closing. Buffalo Bill's show was notably next to the White City (the one that permitted zero urban workhorses) at the Exposition rather than inside. It was not part of the future. If being American was about that very frontier, then the

Annie Oakley with her sharpshooting medals, 1899. (Library of Congress, LCCN 2009631997)

cowgirls were the most American of all, living on the edge of the country and pushing a social frontier of their own. They were manual laborers but not perceived as "too manly," as reporters reassured readers about Daingerfield. They placed themselves in extraordinary danger aboard bucking broncos and riding Roman races with a foot each on two galloping horses. Horses were cowgirls' workmates on the range and costars in the performance arena.

For the many working cowgirls who earned sometimes glancing mentions in the press, partnership with horses cemented their identity. Eighteen-year-old Gertrude Petan reportedly rode the "wildest bronco on the range" in Pratt County, in the territory that became South Dakota. She tended her family's three hundred head of cattle. She pulled stuck cows from mud and wore cowboy clothes: a wide-brimmed felt hat and long gloves. Locals called her the "Lady Cowboy," said the *Chicago Tribune*.[10] When Petan rescued cattle, she did it in "true cowboy fashion."[11]

Bronco Kate, the sixteen-year-old daughter of a cattleman who was raised riding with cowboys, didn't fear the most dangerous horses—even one who kicked and bit. She caught him in his corral, blindfolded him, and rode him until he was tame.[12] (There was lots of blindfolding going on in horse training at the time.) Some cowgirls were more outlaw than diligent rancher. In 1896, a twenty-two-year-old horse thief named Kitty Holm was arrested—wearing men's clothes—in Nez Perce County, Idaho, as part of a gang of four men.[13]

Marcialette "Babe" Walker was eighteen years old and her sister Susie sixteen. Their father, William Walter, hunted bears, and both girls were experts with rifles and "splendid cowgirls," as one article said. They wore cowboy hats, men's coats, calico dresses, wool stockings, and neckerchiefs for riding into town. At home, they wore chaps, overalls, boots, and spurs. They offered a hundred dollars if any man could demonstrate a feat of horsemanship that they couldn't equal, but they hadn't ever had to pay. Susie had ridden to round up a herd of wild horses that ran along a ridge so narrow she couldn't edge past. So, the story went, she galloped over the edge to land nine feet below, stayed on through the whole leap, and turned the herd from there.[14]

Some cowgirls were cast with an outlaw mentality in conjunction with their western equestrianism. The life and death of a woman named Ella Watson merged with those of a legendary figure named Cattle Kate, reputedly the first woman to be hanged in Wyoming. She was about thirty years old and

Sadie Austin on her father's Nebraska ranch, 1900. (Library of Congress, LCCN tmp91001526)

tall, people said, with black hair and eyes and a scar on her chin. When she was riding her buckskin bronco, she wore men's clothes made of corduroy, sometimes with a short skirt, but usually without. She carried a lariat, a knife, and two big revolvers.[15] She habitually "rode through the town like a wild woman," a reporter wrote, "shouting and discharging her revolvers. Now she would shoot at the telegraph poles, and now blaze away at random. The cowboys [sic] were good seconds to her. They did their share of the shooting, and all drank to beat anything."[16]

In reports, Cattle Kate was superhuman until her end, which included a moment of dark horsemanship.[17] When arrested, her partner, James Averill, reportedly whined and claimed innocence, while Kate cursed so much that she couldn't even be gagged. "She called for her own horse to ride to the tree selected for a scaffold and vaulted astride the animal's back from the ground," wrote a reporter. Kate delivered a "blasphemous harangue" to her captors. If the lawmen weren't going to give the herd back, they should sell the herd and donate the money to a home for wayward girls, she said.[18] The lurid headline of the *National Police Gazette* read: "A Blaspheming Border Beauty Barbarously Boosted Branchward."

Riding in the Northwest Plateau. (Library of Congress, LCCN 2018651016)

Cattle Kate wasn't the only supposed female equestrian desperado. Dora Cox, whose aliases included Dora Hawthorn, Darling Nell, Buckskin Nell, and Little Eva, reportedly rode with the legendary Dalton bank-robbing gang. She wore her hair short and wore a man's shirt over a dress, belted with a cartridge holder. She could reputedly hypnotize her jailers. In 1893, the Pawnee Bank of Commerce was robbed by four people in men's clothes. Cox lugged a terrified cashier behind her on her horse as a hostage.[19] Jailed in 1898, she dug her way out with a case knife. "She is neither pretty nor prepossessing but is just as hardened and rough as it would be possible for a woman to become," a reporter wrote. By December, Dora was spotted riding a roan horse, barefoot and in rags.[20]

In March 1902, a woman named Cora Chiquita reportedly shot up a town while drunk and then disappeared. She was twenty-three and wore men's clothes, including a spangled sombrero and a revolver belt around her waist, an article said. A dead-eye shot, she carried a repeating carbine rifle. She presented a puzzle: on the one hand, a good-hearted woman, but on the other, a criminal, "with her wild heart aflame with mingled whisky [*sic*]and wrath." Some thought she was a sort of advance man for train robbers, figuring out the likeliest targets and passing along information to brigand bands.[21] She was a quarter Cherokee and had started riding at seven, roaming from Cherokee territory to the Texas panhandle. She opened a saloon with a man and wore the "nattiest frontier male attire."[22]

Outlaws like Chiquita and the working cowgirls before them morphed, in the public eye, into the performing cowgirl. Around the turn of the century, women competed against men for bronco riding and roping prizes at rodeos. But as time went by, promoters often staged events as exhibitions rather than contests, and women rode against each other in events like Pony Express-style relay racing, trick riding, and bronco riding.[23] At some fairs, women rode in jockey silks, blindfolding horses so they didn't shy at the chaotic scenes in mounting chutes.[24] Legendary bronc rider Fannie Sperry Steele rode in one five-day-long relay in which women changed horses every mile.[25]

Like other horsewomen, cowgirls risked their lives. Performing cowgirl Teresa Russell was practicing for an act in a Wild West show in Vincennes, Indiana, when she leaped from one galloping horse to another. Her foot caught in the stirrup, and she was dragged. "The cowboys made desperate attempts to stop the horses," a reporter wrote, "but were unable to do so until finally one of them stuck a pitchfork into the side of the animal which was dragging Miss Russell, killing it instantly." The ghastly scene of carnage— blades sticking into a dead horse, handle waving, the girl nevertheless lying dead in the arena—highlighted the peril into which performing women placed themselves every day.[26]

A poem that appeared in the *New York Times* in 1897 described the cowgirl's image. One couplet ran: "When she'd spring into the saddle, like the cowboys a la straddle / What a picture of wild recklessness and grace!"[27] The cowgirl had many petitioners but refused to settle down. "Many cowboys sought to win her, but the saucy little sinner / Only laughed to scorn their wild, impassioned pleas." The poem ends with the cowgirl falling in love with a "high-toned" legislator, and the last line is: "And she has to dress up and behave herself." Strangely, the poem seemed to wish the worst for the cowgirl, as if she deserved to be tied up and forced to "behave" after all the broken hearts and feral horses. The title hints at the cowgirl's eventual taming, but as the stanzas escalate the tension surrounding her wildness and freedom, the reader wonders what can happen. Her pleasure, eventually, must end. You couldn't recklessly straddle a saddle forever in 1897.

Lucille Mulhall may have represented the culmination of the working cowgirl morphing into a performer. Her father owned a ranch, and racehorses in St. Louis.[28] He was also the livestock agent for the St. Louis and San Francisco railroad.[29] She could never pinpoint when she started riding but had "lived more or less on horseback ever since she was a little baby," a reporter wrote.[30] Early stories mention that Mulhall's mother opposed her performing men's ranch tasks but decided that supporting it was the patriotic thing to do.[31] Mulhall, wrote one observer, was "not a beauty, such as Titian would have chosen for his masterpieces, but she is a very good specimen of a western girl full of life and health. She is stronger than most men."[32]

The family lived in a town called Mulhall on Beaver Creek, about fifty miles from Oklahoma City. "The Mulhalls are of Southern descent," one reporter wrote, finding a drawing room with loaded bookshelves. "Like her admirer, the President, Miss Mulhall is fond of the strenuous life. She can shoot with the skill of a frontierswoman. . . . She rides astride and boldly. She does not know the meaning of fear. She loves the open air and the plains. Hers has been a life out of doors."[33] Mulhall attributed her riding ability to long rides over open country and felt sorry for girls who didn't live on a ranch and had to stay inside, attending teas.[34]

In 1899, Mulhall won a cowboy race at the Fair Grounds in St. Louis.[35] She was twelve or thirteen but looked grown-up and drew star attention by riding ponies with vicious reputations. She earned "the envy of all the women and, perhaps, half the men." She wasn't pretty, a reporter said. Her hands looked like a cowboy's. She acted "shy and backward" with a stranger. But she shone with horses, wore custom-made boots and tiny silver spurs, and when she rode fast, you could see the narrowest strip of white lace under her skirts.[36]

Roosevelt first "discovered" Mulhall at a reunion of Rough Riders, veterans who had ridden with him in the Mexican-American War. She was fourteen years old. Versions of the story proliferate, but it seems clear that horsemen thrilled to watch her break a bronco, lasso a steer, and shoot a coyote, although Roosevelt visibly paled watching the pony plunge. Afterward, though, he bowed to Mulhall and told her that there wasn't a Rough Rider who could outperform her.[37] According to one account, he asked for her handkerchief that day, while his staff took shiny skirt buttons as souvenirs.[38]

Mulhall, 1909. (Library of Congress, LCCN 00651246)

In another, Roosevelt begged her not to ride a very wild horse who had "wicked, gleaming eyes and dangerous teeth." But Lucille, wearing buckskins, tamed the horse, and "Colonel Roosevelt declared she was the most wonderful horsewoman he had seen on his tour."[39]

Roosevelt told Mulhall that he wanted a wolf but would only accept one that she herself had roped. "You shall have him," she told the then-colonel, and explained to a reporter: "I was riding a good horse—yes, a very good horse—and I said to myself, 'Mr. Wolf, it is all day with you.' . . ." She ran the wolf down, roped him, and then the wolf chewed through the lariat and ran away for another three miles.[40] She sent the pelt off to the Roosevelts at their country home in Oyster Bay, Long Island, and Ethel Roosevelt wrote to say it was in the library there.[41] Association with Roosevelt became a key part of Mulhall's marketing and legend, crafted largely by her father, who retold the stories to reporters, advance men, and promoters.

Mulhall would retell Roosevelt-flavored stories when pressed, but she was at her liveliest talking about her horses. "I wish I had Sam, my favorite pony, here," she said at a 1902 rodeo. "I am going to ride a cowboy's horse which papa [sic] has selected for me. He says it is a good one, but I don't believe it can come up to Sam."[42]

98   ASTRIDE

"Now, Cobb here is one of the best cow horses I ever saw," she said at a later performance, patting his nose. "He has just one fault, and that is a great disadvantage in a roping contest. He starts for a steer as soon as he sees him, like a hound after a rabbit. . . . So I have blindfolded Cobb until I get ready for him to start. Then he is off with a big bound and knows just which side of the flying steer to run on for me to throw my lasso."[43]

Mulhall's Thoroughbred mare, Virgie d'Or, was mistakenly entered in a claiming race, in which every entrant is automatically placed up for sale. Mulhall didn't know and protested when the horse was claimed.[44] When the Mulhalls refused to give the mare over to the rightful new owner, George Hazard, he sued. Mulhall "went to Virgie's stall, stroked the mare's glossy coat, fed her some sugar and cried a little bit." "'He shan't have the mare,'" she said. 'Do you think I am going to let Mr. Hazard or Mr. Anybody Else have Virgie? No, indeed. And they can just tell him so, too.'"[45]

In February 1902, twenty thousand people assembled in Wichita, forming the largest recorded crowd at a roping contest. All stood when Mulhall entered, riding a small bay. Icy rain fell as she repeatedly tried to send her rope around the horns of the most ferocious-looking steer in the herd. The rope, frozen and unwieldy, refused to settle for what seemed like an unbearable time, but she finally landed it around the animal and "pandemonium" ensued. "Men and women shouted themselves hoarse," a reporter wrote, "hats and umbrellas were thrown in the air, air horns blared and it seemed as though the multitude had gone wild."[46]

Days later, Mulhall was riding in a relay race with fifteen thousand spectators. The contestants were racing past the quarter pole, and Mulhall was a little ahead when a rider shot by. His horse's hoof hit her, and she came off.[47] A line sketch of the accident showed Lucille, her hat tossed to the side, under her pony's hooves while the pony, ears back, gallops over her.[48]

"It was time for us to change horses," she said later of the accident. "I made ready to change, but just as I was ready to jump the boy back of me came up. The hoof of his horse struck my ankle. I fell to the ground. Then a policeman came and picked me up." Her boot was torn from her foot, the muscles and tendons of her left ankle ripped away.[49] She loved horses above everything, she told a reporter, who visited her as she rested under a picture of her horse, Petit Maitre, who'd suffered wounds to his own foot in the accident. Mulhall's father teased, asking what her mother would say when she heard Mulhall had been hurt by a horse.[50]

Accounts of this accident demonstrate the usual fascination with horse-women coming to harm, as well as what a celebrity Mulhall had become. Many papers covered the incident. By the next week, she was able to go to San Antonio with her father's group for a roping contest, but only to watch, still fettered by her plaster cast, not unlike Lida Fleitmann Bloodgood, miserably sidelined but watching a horse show at Madison Square Garden.[51]

In 1905, Mulhall was in New York to "show eastern equestriennes a thing or two," in a spectacle very different from Madison Square Garden's usual horse shows, with their hatted society audiences, jumper classes, and hunter paces.[52] The Mulhalls did not like to appear "country." They wore dress clothes and rode in carriages so that the president of the Standard Coach Horse company could show them how trainers worked with Eastern blooded horses.[53] Mulhall had always ridden astride, and, as one reporter wrote, the style was catching: "It may be mentioned that quite recently some of the most popular ladies of New York's exclusive set have given up the sidesaddle and appeared bravely riding astride."[54]

Along with performing cowboys, Mulhall and her sisters tore through Manhattan, riding from Madison Square Garden straight up Fifth Avenue. The cowboys in the group wore chaps and wide-brimmed hats, and the women rode astride. Riderless, Lucille's trick pony had no difficulty weaving through traffic to keep up with the rest. But once the group arrived at Central Park, a mounted officer stopped them. No loose horses allowed. Fortunately, one of the cowboys was close by in a cab, and he hopped on.[55] The group headed north, and at Olmsted's wandering bridle paths, they let their horses run. Even this group of wide-open plains riders couldn't ignore the park's beauty. "I wish Papa could get a piece of it and start a ranch there," said Lucille.[56]

You could hear Zach Mulhall's training when any of the family spoke in public. "There's nothing wonderful in the riding talent of the Mulhall girls," youngest daughter Mildred said in 1910. "It's only a natural gift. . . . I hope to be able to ride a horse as long as I live."[57] A reporter wrote an article about the advantages of the Mulhalls' "natural" way of life that summed their attitude up neatly: "The girl who rides horseback has but herself to please."[58]

In 1903, Zach Mulhall said Lucille, now seventeen, was the best horse-woman in the country.[59] She earned titles from others, too, that often alluded to her in male terms. One headline referred to Mulhall as the Queen of the Cowboys, a different role from "cowgirl," possibly alluding to how many

100   ASTRIDE

coed contests she took. In 1903 an ad for the Congress of Rough Riders of the World advertised Mulhall as "riding cow boy [*sic*] fashion,"[60] and she was called the "president's cowboy friend."[61] "Miss Mulhall does not ride in prim military style, but with the easy, relaxed grace of cattle men," wrote on reporter in 1908.[62]

Trouble seemed to find headstrong, showboating Zach Mulhall, who was arrested at the World's Fair in 1904 for shooting and wounding a stagecoach driver, a cowboy, and a visitor in front of the Cummins Wild West show.[63] Lucille was with her father when he reportedly dared a man named John Reed to shoot him as the two fought. When Reed refused, Zach Mulhall shot Reed twice. The bullets hit others too. Wounded men groaned from the ground, and Zach Mulhall ran off. Police wagons came to the scene, followed by ambulances. Zach returned to turn himself in while Lucille stood by, crying. "He was employed by Colonel Cummins, just as I was," Reed said, "but he tried to boss the whole show. I wouldn't stand for it."[64] Zach Mulhall was released upon bond a little later.[65] Mulhall, for his part, said that he didn't know whose gun had shot the victims. (The dispute apparently stemmed from how much communal feed Zach Mulhall gave his horses.)[66] But he was still convicted and sentenced to three years in jail.[67] Some months later, Lucille Mulhall was listed as a performer at a benefit for families of slain detectives.[68]

With unwholesome stories attached to the Mulhalls, some Oklahomans turned against them. "This statement that Lucille Mulhall is to appear in a wild west scene in New York only exasperates the people of Oklahoma, who dislike advertisements that exaggerate the 'wildness' of Oklahoma," ran one article in the *Guthrie (Oklahoma) Daily Leader*. The paper also mentioned Zach Mulhall's recent shooting. "The Mulhalls do not live in Oklahoma. Their home is in St. Louis. Oklahoma people with their refinement and stature do not know the Mulhalls and an exhibition such as they gave at Fort Worth and would give in New York would be just as much of a novelty to the people of Oklahoma as the people of New York or anywhere in the East," the reporter wrote. "Oklahoma people who attend grand opera . . . are tired of such people who pose as representing Oklahoma."[69]

To these aspirants to refinement, there was something too rough about Lucille too. Perhaps it was her physicality, her cowgirlness, the rowdy image of her drinking in a bar. She was no Thoroughbred trainer or horse show rider. Even though people lined up to watch her, there lingered a note of approbation in how she represented women of the West to the tastemakers of the East. "The sooner we are rid of them the better," wrote one citizen. Another said to remember that "Miss Lucille is not to blame for her actions, as she is made to do things by her father."[70]

Mulhall performed alongside cowboy comedian Will Rogers in 1905. He did rope tricks from his buckskin, and she showed off her horse, Governor, whom she'd trained to walk on his knees.[71] Governor "sat," too, like a giant burro.[72] At one performance, a steer wrenched loose in Madison Square Garden, jumping over a bar that was set at the steps to the street and scrambling up the steps to the second and third balcony steps. Rogers roped the bull by the horns and managed to convince him to return to the ring. Zach shouted to Lucille, asking why she didn't "follow that baby up the stairs and bring him back or else stay there."[73]

As she grew older, Mulhall became more forceful and publicly opinionated. (She also may have been growing weary of the same questions from reporters.) She refused to return a ring to a cowboy who'd thought it would mark their engagement and told the judge in the case that she was used to receiving gifts and didn't see why she should give it back. Many people paid her compliments that way, she said, including the president.[74] She secretly married Martin Van Bergen, a vaudeville singer, in October 1908, but the marriage did not last.[75]

In 1910, a reporter asked if Mulhall found her long skirt hard to ride in. "I have always worn long skirts ever since I was old enough to," she said. "I have seen most 'cowgirls' wear short skirts in Wild West shows, but out in my part of the country the young woman all wear long skirts. . . . I want my exhibition to be real and short skirts are not real on a ranch girl." Did she always ride astride? "I have never rode in any other way," she said. "Of course, we wear divided skirts. We have to. All the girls I know ride astride, as it is the only sensible way for a woman to ride. I think it is the most unnatural thing in the world for a woman to ride sideways. It is so injurious, as well as awkward and unsafe. The few girls I have known who ride in side saddles [*sic*] become perfect freaks by the way in which they develop the right side."[76]

In these later years, there were more dressage performances and fewer bronco rides.[77] A 1917 pageant included Lucille doing a lot of "fancy stepping" on her big gray, Eddie C. Mulhall, still billed as the "the most expert horsewoman in the world," married and divorced again.[78] An ad Mulhall placed in 1916 termed herself the "girl ranger," and said she would furnish any size troupe of roughriders.[79] She was reputedly the first cowgirl to hire other cowgirls for her own riding shows. By 1922, Zach Mulhall was tooling around his ranch on a horse named Charley Sharp, supposedly the last horse Roosevelt had ever mounted, a lingering reminder of the connection that brought the family its fame.[80]

Zach Mulhall died in 1931.[81] "Something fine has passed with the old life," Lucille told a reporter. "This new day is probably fine, too, but I loved the unfenced range and the open prairie and the boundless friendliness of the cattle country."[82]

Some less-famous cowgirls were described with much the same vocabulary as Mulhall. Like Mulhall's, Oregonian Minnie Austen's experience came from her background. (Her father was a horse dealer.) "From a toddler I have been used to riding," she said, "and I presume that it is my constant association with horses that has given me the confidence that makes me believe I can stick to any horse that can be brought to me." She worked for cattle sellers in Portland as a cowgirl, riding the range to bring in herds. In her performances, she'd lash two horses to go as fast as possible over jumps while she rode both.[83] "It is exciting and perhaps dangerous," she said, "but no horse yet has thrown me, and I have had sufficient experience to assure me that I can tame the worst of them."[84]

Horse training itself seemed different out West, according to May Lillie, the wife of Pawnee Bill, who ran one of the big three Wild West shows. Training focused on partnership more than the skills outlined at a riding academy or in an instructional manual. "The trouble with the American girls of today, who are anxious to become expert riders, is that they do not start right," she said. "They start with their riding habits instead of starting with their horse. It is absolutely necessary to become acquainted with your horse and let your horse become acquainted with you." In this respect, she defined western horsewomanship against eastern styles. Riders who dressed in corsets appalled her. Lillie had roped and backed her own mustang, who was referred to as "May Lillie's Tang."[85] "Horses are like people," she told a reporter in 1906. "Some are intelligent and learn easily, and in others you have to develop the brain for them."[86]

Minnie Thompson, who worked for Buffalo Bill's Wild West show, rode her Arab horse Virgil with no bridle or bit. One day, she went out to Central Park—just behind the Metropolitan Museum of Art—to perform. Soon, a traffic jam developed, as pedestrians, police officers, and Sunday-dressed

Riders in Los Angeles, 1910. (Library of Congress, LCCN 2014691057)

A cowgirl in the streets of Newton, Kansas, in 1908. (Library of Congress, LCCN 2014682206)

parkgoers watched the horse stand on his hind legs, pick up a handkerchief, and walk on his hind legs while she leaned all the way back, her head resting on his rump. Finally, the traffic police asked her to stop. She obeyed and put Virgil's bridle back on. One lady asked how much Thompson wanted for the horse. She shook her head. He wasn't for sale.[87]

Princess Wenona rode with the 101 Ranch's Wild West Show. The daughter of a Sioux leader and a white woman, a reporter wrote in 1911, Princess Wenona was the best shot and horseback rider of her community.[88] (She sometimes used the alias Lillie Smith, wrote another reporter.)[89] She could shoot as well from a galloping pony as when she was standing.[90] One show advertised this as "performing amazing feats of marksmanship while astride a wild horse."[91] A photograph shows Wenona riding a horse in braids and a shawl or cape; the horse wears a rope or hide bridle.[92] In another, she presses her face to her horse's cheek; she wears a headdress, and this horse also wears the lightest of halters, tied with bows, suggesting the expertise required to guide him.[93] Wenona died in 1930, and according to an article from that year, after years spent performing with various shows, she bought her own Oklahoma farm, where she raised goats, chickens, and geese.[94]

Cowgirl Fannie Sperry Steele moved from relay races to bronco busting, a contest of endurance on a bucking horse. This started when cowboys would simply ride horses until they were "broken" or "busted." In 1905, Steele mounted a bucking bronco named Tracy, who launched her over his head. She twisted miserably in the air before she smashed into the ground. People in the audience screamed. But she was unaccountably all right.[95]

Some women bronc riders "hobbled" their stirrups, meaning that they tied them together. This kept the rider more firmly in the saddle and prevented her legs from clanging into the horse's sides. But judges preferred riders to ride "slick and clean," and Steele, along with Bertha Blancett and Tillie Baldwin, rode that way.[96] In 1912, Steele won the championship at the Calgary Stampede, and by 1914, she and her husband traveled with their own Wild West show with horses, performers, and a chuck wagon in which they camped as they rode along. Steele rode broncos, performed speed events, and shod her own horses. An urban reporter was so shocked by this that he wrote, instead, that she "showed" horses, believing he must have misunderstood.[97]

New Yorker Tillie Baldwin became the first woman to win a Roman race, in which a standing rider plants a foot each on two galloping horses. "You hold on with the lower part of the thigh, being careful to keep the legs curved in, so that the calves cling to the animal's flanks," she explained. "And you don't try to sit erect in your saddle. I lean back and keep my chin down, so that when the animal bucks, he doesn't jerk my head back and hurt my neck."[98] In an eight-day rough-riding contest—essentially riding untamed broncos—at Sheepshead Bay, Brooklyn, she won over Westerners.[99]

By 1911, the generic cowgirl was sometimes burlesqued as masculine and demanding. One story told of an Easterner who went west to marry a cowgirl, only to have his new wife point a gun at him when she wanted him to wash the dishes.[100] Others laughed at the stereotype; rider Kitty Canutt reputedly had two gold incisors set with diamonds.[101]

The stereotype may have some origin from the spectacle of cowgirls who rode bucking horses, an astonishing tough and athletic feat. Cheyenne's Frontier Days was probably the first of the giant, somewhat theatrical operations to feature cowgirls aboard broncos, and Oregon's Pendleton Round-Up also

Kitty Canutt in Wyoming, riding a bronco named Winnemucca, 1919. (Library of Congress, LCCN 90708943)

showcased a group of "lass ropes," sometimes wearing fringed buckskins.[102] The Round-Up, a sort of combination pageant and sporting event, took place every fall to commemorate and mythologize the pioneer days of the "Wild West."[103]

For something based on wildness, there were plenty of rules. You couldn't hand the rope from one hand to the other. You had to swing your legs from the horse's shoulder to rear and fan your hat fully. You said, "Going up!" when mounting. There was no touching the horn with either hand.[104] Cowgirls who wanted to ride broncos needed to be proven horsewomen, but any cowboy could ride. "In this contrast is an interesting phase of the psychology of the crowd, who dearly love to see a cowboy bucked off, but take no delight in seeing a cowgirl go the same way," wrote Charles W. Furlong in his 1913 *Let 'Er Buck*.[105]

Performers worked hard to fulfill an audience's idea of what a cowgirl was. Mabel Strickland was twenty-one in 1918, a bit younger than Mulhall and in the wake of her influence. She did the basics like standing and vaulting, and audiences loved her signature moves atop her Arabian mare Buster. She traveled beneath her galloping horse's belly or stood up and leaned backward, miming swigging whiskey while her horse raced underneath her. She jumped Buster over a car.[106] She did everything with a dancer's flair; one photograph shows her grinning to the crowd from beneath the brim of her dark cowboy hat mid-leap, one foot in the stirrup, while her horse, mid-gallop, has only one foot on the ground.[107] She went on to perform on-screen and cofounded the Association of Film Equestriennes in 1934.[108]

A cowgirl named Margaret Portelyou wanted to ride Dynamite, a downcast-looking horse who'd drawn a milk wagon, but he hated to be ridden, according to a newspaper story. He had thrown four cowboys when she decided to ride him. "You didn't give me a wedding present, Bert," she told her new husband. "Let me try just once to ride Dynamite, and if he throws me I'll be satisfied." Her husband said no, so she asked if she could just have her picture taken with the horse. Once she was next to him, posing, she jumped on his back. People flew, but she stuck on while the horse leaped and bucked.[109]

Lorena Trickey, a Wyoming cowgirl, told a reporter that she didn't like that in New York,

> one can't get out in the middle of the street and yell if one just happens to feel that way. My; how everybody would stare. Then a policeman would come up and move you along and want to know why you did that and what was the matter with you and how you got that way. That is the difference between New York and the far west between saying right out what one feels and going about with a bored face. What strikes me most about New York is the air of make-believe that is just chronic with folks that have lived here long. They just can't put real "pep" into life.[110]

In 1909, fifteen-year-old Celia Corbetoff ran away from her home in Washington, DC. (There was a warrant out for her. The charge: "being incorrigible.") "You know I'm going back to Washington just for a day," she told the detectives who found her in Baltimore, "then I am going out on the plains. I'm going to be a cowboy. You fellows are too timid to me, so go ahead—fire your questions." The detectives wanted her to say where she'd been for the past month, but she was more interested in laying out plans. "If I had on my buckskins, with my gun, as I will have when I get out West, I would make some of you fellows dance some," she said. "Don't you know that in the West there is real life."[111]

108   ASTRIDE

Corbetoff was responding to the spirit of the cowgirl. "In these women is represented a resourceful self-reliance, yet they are intensely feminine withal," writes Furlong.[112] That was the Annie Oakley goal: the independence of the West, with the "intense" femininity Americans still prized. In November 1902, the eight "bachelor girl" daughters of an Oregon rancher worked outdoors wearing duck, buckskin, and calico. They trained horses and slept outside. "Withal these daring bachelor girls are quiet-mannered and womanly and they are only unmarried because every one of them is in love with their present lot," wrote a reporter.[113] This summed up the cowgirl ethos. The "bachelor girls," notably termed with a male-centered word—could have been married. They were fitting enough to exist inside society's most typical sphere—but they didn't want to be. They were already in love.

The performing cowgirl's cousins, circus riders, also worked within a world designed to show them off. Sequined and bejeweled, they created such spectacles with their riding that they almost hid the athleticism on exhibition. Like the cowgirls, circus riders captivated audiences, embodying something novel, stirring, and bold.

6

Circus Riders

Horses really make a circus.[1] Shakespeare refers to a "dancing horse" in *Love's Labor Lost*.[2] Cavalryman Philip Astley, the "father of the modern circus," performed in a field near London's Westminster Bridge in the seventeenth century, recreating chariot races.[3] In America, historian Les Standiford writes, audiences saw "high-riders" as early as 1771, and at the circus George Washington attended in 1793—the same day he issued the Proclamation of Neutrality clarifying the United States' position in terms of a war between France and England—a horsewoman performed.[4]

In her series of articles about the *écuyères* or "transgressive horsewomen" of the nineteenth-century Parisian circus, Susanna Forrest writes that they lived "at the center of public attention while simultaneously being marginal. They dealt with racism, misogyny, abuse, and great physical danger but, like the circus, they endured."[5] In America in the years from 1890 to 1925, circus women lived with a similar insider-outsider tension. They were the beating heart of the circus, but society kept them in their rings. Like the *écuyères*, they stayed.

Horsewomen amplified the circus's spectacle, combining danger and beauty, fire, spangles, and light. Circuses transported audiences by disrupting the everyday. Lion-tamers and wild animals paired with horses, forming a tableau of human dominance over animals while maintaining visual wildness. Beauty, equine and human, propelled the awe that made audiences re-see the world during a performance, and marginalize circus women in society. They weren't quite "real" to most people. Around the turn of the twentieth century, their performances celebrated the period's obsession with flight. In a country gripped by airborne, imperiled aviatrixes, circus women somersaulted and leaped so much they appeared suspended above their churning, snorting horses. Others were hoisted, mounted, aloft by a hot-air balloon. "The new woman has invaded the circus ring," said one article in 1896. "There isn't a single pink tulle skirt in the new circus."[6]

Buffalo Bill Cody once socked a peeping Tom who was peering into a women's tent, which highlights the danger circus women lived with as they forged new ground.[7] As Janet Davis writes in her *Circus Age*, "The mobile circus was a staging ground in which multiple shifting American attitudes about gender, race, and the female body were negotiated and contested at the turn of the century."[8]

Circuses ran on trains, pulling up to towns and unloading animals, car by car, as townspeople lined sidewalks to watch them parade to fairgrounds. As early as 1872, Barnum, Coup, and Costello's circuses traveled the country, and by 1897 Barnum & Bailey's Greatest Show on Earth owned its own sixty-foot cars. By 1910, about three dozen circuses were chugging across American railroads.[9]

Advance men rolled posters onto walls (real estate owners received tickets in exchange) with a flour-and-water paste. Circus advertising often consisted of gorgeous, florid images of horsewomen. Bareback rider May Wirth smiles from a 1910 poster, wearing a pink bow in her hair, ballet shoes, and a brief, pink outfit. She has her white horse by the bridle. With his back left and front right feet off the ground, and his neck arched, he embodies an animal only manageable by someone of Wirth's skill, as her two-handed hold suggests.[10] Another, from 1917, shows Wirth in a French blue ensemble, wearing gold garters, her shoulders bare and her hair worn loose under a blue headband. She beams down from her white horse at a clown who holds his hat in his hand. She holds a riding crop, and although she perches aside, her horse seems in motion, with a ducked head and flared nostrils. She represents something daring, challenging, and powerful.[11]

Workers hauled tents up on ropes, and cages holding animals bore signs warning people not to touch. Others made sure that the performers, including horses, would have enough food, and that local trains could get spectators to the circus.[12] In 1919, there were more than seven hundred horses in the country's biggest circus, Ringling Brothers and Barnum & Bailey Greatest

Crowds line up at the main entrance for a Ringling Brothers circus, ca. 1895–1910. (Library of Congress, LCCN 2016812097)

Show on Earth. Two hundred fifty grooms, drivers, and assistants worked with the show. The circus veterinarian had four assistants, who knew every horse by name.[13]

Horses rode to circus settings on trains. A "wedge horse" helped the others load. (He "wedged" himself in last, and then was the first one out, convincing the other horses that they were safe.) Then the wagon horses worked, hauling structures from the circus setting to the train car, while the circus horses took a rest until rehearsal time.[14] Bareback riders' horses wore only a surcingle around their bellies and sometimes, a bridle. They were called "rosinbacks" because performers used rosin (plant-based resin in a solid form) to improve friction between their feet and horsehide.[15] Some said that circus horses were purposefully kept fat, with the idea that the extra heft would make them less likely to bolt.[16]

Going to the circus—sneaking in was called "sidewalling"—meant that you bought a ticket, often at a red ticket wagon. Next, you'd gather popcorn, peanuts, ice cream, or lemonade, before heading under the canvas tent for the show. If you walked around the performers' quarters, you might catch some household scenes, like a woman hanging tights out to dry on the guy ropes of a tent.[17] Inside the tents, women performers sat on canvas director's chairs in front of trunks containing costumes and listened for musical cues.[18] Rider Madame Marantette combed her Maltese's hair while she waited to ride. Ernestine Rose Meers mended lavender tights. Near showtime, they buttoned each other's outfits up the back.[19]

In Margaret Mayo's 1908 novel *Polly of the Circus*, a clown and circus manager raise a young girl after her mother dies in a riding accident. Polly's talent is obvious from the moment she climbs onto a Shetland pony's back and starts dancing.[20] Although wildly skilled, she's overconfident, just like her doomed mother, and the kindly men who raise her beg her not to do "extra stunts."[21] "There ain't no act so hard as a ridin' act," she says, her dialect demonstrating the folksy, uneducated nature of circus people.[22] When Polly gets hurt, after much foreshadowing, she must stay in a small-town pastor's home to recuperate. "'Do you expect to have our young folks associatin' with a circus ridin' girl?'" a town deacon asks her guardian.[23] Eventually, Polly herself grows sheepish about her past, when, to her now-shame, she rode through public streets in tights. In despair when she believes the parson won't marry her, she attempts suicide by horse.

Polly suffers because of her transgressive position, which some real circus women did too. In 1903, Sells Brothers bareback rider Estelle Wainwright found herself in a jail hospital after overdosing on morphine and whiskey. She'd been hurt in Baltimore around 1900, she said. She couldn't work again, started the morphine because her injury hurt so much, and wound up addicted and "in a wretched condition," forced outside any societal safety nets.[24]

Perhaps because of situations like Wainwright's, circus women emphasized the healthy and wholesome nature of their lives to reporters whenever they could. A reporter went to see seventeen-year-old Josephine Clarke as she learned a new trick in 1913. She was wearing trunks and a blue sweater, and a rope fastened to her belt led to a pulley overhead. A man held a long lead line while she rode. "Do you know," she said, "it may interest some of the people who are good enough to applaud our efforts that this is just the happiest, healthiest sort of life a girl can live. Why, I've been practicing here

A bareback rider standing outside a tent with her horses, ca. 1904. (Library of Congress, LCCN 90712947)

114   ASTRIDE

since 7 o'clock this morning and now I feel like going out and eating another breakfast." She was an outdoorsy and wholesome horsewoman, not a spangly actress-type of person, she indicated. Clarke did not want people to see her as Polly of the Circus, itinerant or needing redemption.[25]

Trainers worked new circus horses in rings surrounded by hay bales, forcing the horses to canter on a "track." Once the horses were able to gallop on a circle at a consistent pace, trainers removed the hay, bale by bale, focused on maintaining the rhythm that riders needed for tricks. Then, riders were held by a swivel-jointed belt to a pulley mechanism.[26] A line ran through the ring over the horse's back to a trainer's hands. The horse would travel in a circle, with the apparatus above him, and the trainer would urge the horse to go or to halt. Before this machinery, a rider would train above straw mattresses in case of falling, but with it, the rider could pause in the air, swinging from the crane, and then "dismount" whenever she wanted.[27]

Riding acrobats learned to fall, pulling themselves into a tight ball as soon as they hit the ground. They also learned to control their bodies even when in midair, when they could gauge the horse's position underneath them. To slow down, they lifted their heads a bit, and to speed up, they bent more fully. In the worst cases, riders trained themselves to "hit the horse," meaning they could get close enough to push off the horse's body with a foot and control the landing. In 1895, a reporter asked a male circus rider if anyone had tried a double somersault. "I don't think so," the man replied, "and I am very sure no one has ever succeeded. You know a single somersault on a horse's back is no joke, and was done for the first time by the merest accident. . . . I should hate to try a double on a horse."[28]

But that double somersault—"no joke"—would become May Wirth's signature. Wirth, an Australian by birth, became an American sensation. At times, she was the highest salaried performer in the circus.[29] Ringling Brothers named one of their bears after her.[30] Her adoptive mother worked as ringmistress, and she rode with her brother, a clown who performed with a kangaroo.[31]

Wirth traveled with fourteen Arabians and Australian stock horses, and she switched mounts often during her performance so that they didn't get dizzy.[32] One of her horses, Snow, had pulled a hearse in Dayton but lost his job to a motorized hearse. She named another Peggy (for Pegasus).[33] "They are more human than many human beings," said Wirth, "and they understand me just as I understand them."[34] Was she ever scared? "Me afraid?" she said. "Pooh! I was born on Friday, the 13th, and I firmly believe it has proved a lucky boon for me all through life."[35] Even as a small child, she could climb poles and instinctively roll away from approaching hooves. "I start to spring through the air at just the second or part of a second when the little watch inside me says it's time to go," she said. "That's the only watch we riders have and the only one we ever need."[36]

Wirth pleaded with a family friend and horse trainer to let her spend the day with horses by the time she was around seven, she said. She started performing at ten.[37] Wirth practiced bareback for hours at a stretch, refusing even to use a pad. She was the first woman to turn somersaults while a horse galloped.[38] To teach herself the somersaults, she first used a bag of bran shaped like a horse's back, to gauge where to take off and land. The ring was usually the same size—the horses took twenty-one paces to go around—and the upward motion of the canter gave her a trampoline for the somersaults.[39] Her leaps from the ground were "flat," meaning that she didn't use running boards or any kind of stool on the takeoff.[40]

By sixteen, Wirth was touring the country with Barnum & Bailey. Take a break, her mother pleaded, but instead, Wirth begged for a horse to ride in the circus. "I am not happy away from my horse," she said.[41] One, Joe, was a ten-year-old part Arabian, who she'd bought from a fellow rider, Josephine Demott, for $1,000, about $28,000 today. Joe liked Madison Square Garden, but across the river to Brooklyn, he grew too spooky and Wirth had to use another horse for her act, which she felt "quite bad" about.[42] "To become a first-class rider," she said, fixing her hat, about to go into the ring, "a girl must be very fond of animals, and must love to ride better than do anything else in the world."[43] She wasn't even a tiny bit frightened? "I never felt afraid on a horse in my life," said Wirth.[44] She believed Joe was a reincarnation of a soldier from the heraldic era. On one transatlantic journey on an Italian ship, passengers tried to feed him spaghetti.[45]

Like Elizabeth Daingerfield, Wirth didn't particularly like to talk except about horses. She was oddly clumsy on the ground, tripping and falling over her own feet. Her mother said she was safest on horseback, but Wirth attributed her success to knowing how to fall.[46] She was five feet tall, muscular, and credited her health to riding. "It is an exercise that keeps one feeling fine all the time," she said. "Even in hot weather, when one is apt to feel loggy

116   ASTRIDE

[*sic*] and lazy, as soon as I get on my horse and go through some exercises, I feel fit for anything."[47]

On opening night during one New York engagement, Wirth entered through a double line of mounted men, who assembled in an homage-paying manner. Next, she leaped from the ground to a standing pose on her horse. She turned somersaults at full speed and did a "back across," where she back-flipped from one horse to another, rotating in the air.[48]

By 1913, Wirth headlined Barnum & Bailey's circus. On April 22, soon after the season opener, Wirth had completed the trick to tremendous applause—this was what the audience had come to see—and was lying across the back of Juno, her white part Arabian, in the center ring.[49] She bowed to the crowd. Her right foot was in a rope stirrup fastened to the horse's side (it was used by circus attendants to hang onto the horse during a moment in the act), and she hung, head down, on his left side as he cantered around the ring. She sat up for a moment, slipped, and then fell. Normally, Wirth could land on her knees or on her feet on the ground. But this time, her foot was stuck. Juno kept cantering, trained to maintain a steady pace. Wirth's head bounced "like a shuttlecock," wrote one reporter, thumping as the horse went around on the tanbark four times. Her head barely missed Juno's churning hooves and hit the wooden rim at the bottom of the ring. The band played on. Attendants caught the horse, but he escaped. Finally, they caught hold of him and carried Wirth out of the tent. Some thought the event was part of the show until they saw blood drip from a gash over her right ear. Gasping audience members fled, believing they'd just watched her die.[50] But the next day Wirth was recovering. She had a concussion and bruising, the circus's doctor said, but no broken bones, and no internal injuries.[51] She'd be laid up for several weeks.[52] A report of the accident appeared on the front page of the *New York Times* under the headline, "May Wirth Badly Hurt," no identification, a testament to her celebrity.[53]

She was hurt again later in the year in St. Louis.[54] "May Wirth has the courage of Ulysses, the stamina of Prometheus," wrote one reporter. Even on vacation she rode every day.[55] In 1919, Wirth still somersaulted backward through rings and leaped from the ground to her galloping spotted horse.[56] (There was some possibly deliberate confusion about her age. She was called nineteen in 1919, a bit tricky if she was sixteen in 1912.)[57] The idea of a rider as a young girl in constant danger added some interest to her act. She wore gingham rompers when she wasn't riding.

Circus Riders   117

In one performance, Wirth followed a stage appearance by Helen Keller.[58] She performed several times in front of Woodrow Wilson (the Secret Service had to talk him down from riding an elephant) and gave a demonstration to the King of England. Wirth liked a crowd filled with children best.[59] "When the face is relaxed in a smile all the rest of the body relaxes, too," she said. "And so, you see, I always land on my feet."[60]

Attorney Jess Kelley, who represented circus people, had heard Wirth say she could ride anything on four feet, so he dared her to ride his three-year-old, two-ton bull King at his farm in Hackensack, New Jersey. Celebrities gathered to witness the challenge: a Rough Rider named Howard Tegland, champion cyclist Alfred Goulette, and baseball legend Babe Ruth. Wirth wore riding pants instead of her usual tights. Ruth rode too. A photographer snapped pictures of them both.[61] Ruth, wearing a three-piece suit and a striped tie, waves his hat from atop King, Holstein-spotted. He's grinning, but his legs are back and he's gripping hard.[62] In her photo, Wirth does a handstand. She's wearing a tweed jacket and tweed pants with high riding boots, looking like a country lady, her hair neatly parted, but her feet wave high in the air and she smiles while she poses on the bull's back.[63]

In May, circus owner Johnny Ringling went to the White House, and invited President Calvin Coolidge to a Washington, DC, performance. Coolidge loved horses and circuses, and as a young boy, had left home before dawn to ride to Rutland, Vermont, when the circus was in town. On a Tuesday in May, the band played "Hail to the Chief," as the Coolidges crossed the circus ring. Parents tried to point out the president to their children, but they were too excited by the circus to care. Coolidge watched the show in wonder. "He gave it his undivided attention," a reporter wrote, "as if cramming into this one afternoon all the circuses he mussed in the trying, busy years of his political career." Ringling finally gave up trying to talk to him. But it wasn't until May Wirth appeared, smiling and bowing before the presidential box, that the famously laconic president actually smiled.[64]

Later in her career, Wirth kept trying to retire, but instead, she was, as she said, "continually playing farewell performances."[65] She was enshrined in the Circus Hall of Fame in 1964 and died in 1978.[66]

Rose Wentworth started riding with the circus in 1894, and became the second rider, after Wirth, to perform a somersault from horseback. She was from Fall River, Massachusetts, and married a clown at sixteen.[67] In one performance,

118   ASTRIDE

Circus at Coney Island, ca. 1910–1915. (Library of Congress, LCCN 2014689475)

Wentworth raced a chariot, rode as a jockey and did contortions, squeezing herself through a small ring.[68] In another, called "Rose Wentworth's Horses," Harry pretended to be a bumbling stable boy, and in her "champagne" act, she pretended to be drunk and sway as the horse galloped beneath her.[69] A reporter once asked what she thought of circus life. She liked it, she said. The women needlepointed and held running races when the performance was over.[70]

By 1905 she was performing as "The Rose Wentworth Equestrian Sensation," entering in a small carriage pulled by Arabian horses and working toward a double bareback exhibition.[71] "There are no women equestriennes that excel her in graceful and daring feats," wrote a reporter in 1905.[72] Wentworth appeared on a bill with Harry Houdini in 1906 and on one with a trained "laughing" horse.[73] That same year, Wentworth planned to retire to her Maine farm, but couldn't bring herself to do it. "Talk about the difficulty experienced by some men and women to break off the habit of drinking liquor," she said. "It isn't a circumstance to the breaking off from. A circus life. Just about the time the trees are beginning to leave and the scent of flowers is in the air, I feel a desperate longing to rove over the country with the circus."[74]

So, Wentworth didn't "break off," even when Harry died in 1909.[75] She remarried a South Dakota rancher in 1912 and continued life in the public eye as Rose Wentworth Carr. She offered to ride the wildest horse anyone could bring to the Calgary Stampede.[76] She also kept a string of wild horses and tamed buffalo in front of crowds.[77] Wentworth traveled with her bison, taking three with her to Argentina so they could perform with a 101 Ranch company. One became sick and died while there, and she tried to bring the other two home, but there was a Bureau of Animal Industry law against importing ruminants from South America at the time. The bison would have to be quarantined and then shot if they showed signs of infection. Wentworth could not understand "why one bureau of the United States should wish to destroy animals that another bureau is trying to preserve."[78] She stayed newsworthy.

Myrtle Peek and Emma Peek, also known as Madame Marantette, sisters from Mendon, Michigan, performed at circuses, racetracks and horse shows.[79] As girls, they entertained crowds at county fairs with their fast bareback riding.[80] One night, Peek arrived late to San Francisco with an exhibition to give the next day. She was exhausted and dusty, but because there were so many people staying at her hotel, she couldn't get a room with a tub. All she saw was an immovable washstand. Peek plugged up the sink, turned on the water, and bathed. Everything went fine, she said, until she became a little excited about the upcoming races, and splashed her feet, imagining that she was straddling two horses as she did in her act. The sink crashed; splintering plaster cut her. Blood and water poured onto the floor. A doctor stitched Peek, and ordered her not to ride, but she didn't obey, and more blood streamed over the horses are she rode them Roman style.[81]

"To be successful in training horses you must manage them exactly as a sensible woman manages her husband," Marantette, the far more famous of the sisters, told the *Chicago Daily Tribune* in 1897. She'd already set one record by then, sailing her horse Filemaker over a seven-foot, three-and-a-half-inch jump in Chicago. Marantette was superstitious and wouldn't begin any work on a Friday.[82] Her name came from an early first marriage, which was annulled; her second was to promoter Daniel Hunt Harris.[83] She believed riding astride was undignified and wore an Austrian-made habit and fedora.[84] Tiffany made her favorite brooch, which depicted her on her high school horse Evergreen. One reporter called her "the Bernhardt of the circus arena," and like Sarah Bernhardt, Marantette understood her audience.[85] Also, like Bernhardt, her understanding of her own image—a romantic-sounding name, bespoke jewelry—translated to outsize, generous performances. Marantette went big.[86]

Her horse Evergreen, for example, had fourteen different gaits. His distinct, dancelike motions exhibited athleticism and training. Marantette's training philosophy sounds very much like that of today's horse expo trainers: "If they are good they get sugar; if they are stubborn they get the whip—but little of the last. Horses are very like men. Sometimes they must be humored and made to think they are having their own way, when in reality they are doing what you will they shall do."[87] Marantette believed that all great jumpers had to be at least half-Thoroughbred, for courage.[88] She'd bought the high-jumping Filemaker sour, sunburned, and fearful, she said. "I love the old fellow for the way he has carried me over the bars, and I believe it will be many a day before another horse and rider equals us in our championship of the world."[89]

At her training operation, Marantette owned a ring barn (an indoor arena). She had a jump set up with poles and pins to raise and lower the hurdle to train horses to the high jump. She worked horses on the Michigan roads.[90] "I would rather have a horse that has had no other training, and I can handle any horse by using kindness and firmness," she said. "I get very fond of a horse if I can make anything of him."[91]

Marantette took some bad falls, including a head injury so severe that she required surgery. Evergreen, hitched to a cart, had turned too fast, and Marantette—"foolishly," as she said later—kept ahold of the reins. She was dragged, knocking her head on an iron step. Her beribboned white Maltese, Ernestine, was thrown then and was temporarily blinded. She began driving again as soon as she could. She worried she'd lost her nerve, because whenever Evergreen lifted his heels, she quaked.[92]

Even after an accident took place, Marantette believed in continuing the high jump. She blamed other riders for approaching the situation wrong-headedly, rushing at the jump when they should allow the horse to gauge his own distance. "They take the horse back three times the distance from the jump they should, head him for the jump at a race-horse clip under such headway and so anxious to get away from the punishment that he has no time to gauge himself and measure his take-off. Then if he falls they blame the horse," she said.[93] She didn't carry a whip on Filemaker, because if he were allowed to go slowly, he'd measure his takeoff and use "more judgment than when he rushes."[94]

In 1903 Marantette was earning a hundred dollars a week, top pay and the same, according to one article, as Wentworth and Ella Bradna, a rider with top billing in 1909 in the Ringling Brothers' circus.[95] (Clowns earned twenty-five dollars; sideshow performers, fifteen dollars.) Living expenses were covered by the tents and the cooking provided.[96] By 1918, Marantette was a multiple record-holder. She'd held the one for the high jump horses since 1891 Filemaker died in 1896. Senator, her next high jumper, couldn't go over seven feet, but St. Patrick, her next, made a record of seven feet, ten and a quarter inches.[97]

St. Patrick liked to refuse the first several times he was shown a high jump, and each time, Marantette rode patiently back to the starting place. She still never used a whip. "Gentleness is the only way to manage St. Patrick or any other horse and I never force him to take the jumps," she said. "The jump is not going to be made until he feels he can go over, and everything is left with him. He holds the world's record and I will not try to break that unless some other horse raises it higher yet."[98]

She'd considered retiring but never stuck with it. She loved performing too much. "But each fall I could not resist the call of riding, and I began to consider why I should retire if I could go on doing as well and better than I had previously. Now I am determined to ride until there is nothing of me,"[99] she said. She died of pneumonia in 1922. Marantette's will reportedly specified that her horse and dog should be buried with her. There aren't accounts of this happening, but being buried with animals is a poignant, ancient idea, full of pomp.[100]

Marantette understood how to be royalty.

In April 1912, May Wirth attended a meeting of suffragists and circus women at the Women's Political Union with her mother and her sister Stella. Suffrage leader Annie Tinker "talked horse with the circus women."[101] By the time of the meeting, The Suffragette Ladies of the Barnum & Bailey Circus had eight hundred members. Josephine Demott, a club president, lived on Long Island, training circus horses. "The circus women live in a little world of their

122   ASTRIDE

own, roaming all over this country, and sometimes in other countries, until age or an accident knocks them out. . . . We discuss the laws of the different States we visit. From these debates we feel sure there is no one who needs this franchise more than ourselves," said Demott. A non-circus leader said that when she saw Katie Sandine hoist three men at a time in her strong woman act, she realized that suffrage should be "an old story" for circus women.[102] They could throw men around; why not vote like them?

On April 30, 1912, suffrage-minded circus women gathered around a baby giraffe they'd named "Miss Suffrage." The giraffe fidgeted when Wirth entered her pen. Nearby, a gnu roared as bulbs flashed.[103] Inez Milholland disappointed the circus women with her absence, so Demott headed to the Women's Political Union, which was on East Twenty-Ninth Street, to fetch some activists. They were busy, but reporters trailed Demott back to the circus, where she made a speech, telling women, "You want to establish clearly in the mind of your husband that you are his equal. You are not above him, but his equal." As she spoke, a man came to remove his wife and daughter from the assemblage. "You are not slaves," Demott shouted at the departing crowd.[104]

The balloon horse stood still, a female rider on his back. Amid fireworks, pulleys lifted him aloft on a platform where a hot-air balloon basket would normally be.[105] The act depended upon the era's obsession with aviation as much as loving horses. Standing calmly while a platform ascended and fireworks cascaded demonstrated an act of extraordinary training and horsemanship. The quiet majesty of horse and rider in the air stunned audiences so much that in at least one instance, a clown lampooned it, pretending to ride a balloon horse. The same fireworks went off, and the same platform dropped, but a safety rope caught the clown, which underlined the hazard of the original act.[106]

Josephine Demott (who held the suffrage meeting) was born into a French circus family and traveled America in circus wagons with her parents and seven siblings. Her father led his children in a regime of everyday calisthenics when Demott wasn't yet five.[107] Every winter, the children went to school in Frankford, Pennsylvania, while simultaneously practicing riding and sewing costumes.[108] By the time Demott joined Barnum & Bailey, her contract specified that every performance had to include three somersaults from a horse in

Circus Riders   123

motion, a trick William T. Aymar died trying to perform.[109] Mexican president Porfirio Diaz gave her a silver laurel leaf as a token of thanks.[110]

Demott, who was married to circus manager Charlie Robinson, wrote a first-person piece for the *New York Times* in 1906.[111] Most circus riders were born or married into the life, she wrote. She emphasized the "tea tables" owned by circus ladies; they were, the piece implied, just as refined as others.[112] She said that loving horses was part of her passion for the circus. She practiced every day but struggled during breaks. "When riding along at a canter," she said, she longed for "the excitement and spice of bareback riding in the ring."[113]

Demott and her horse, also named Charlie, left the circus. She and her husband turned to adventuring, becoming stranded above the Arctic Circle at one point. Next, they headed to Alaska to prospect for gold.[114] That also ended badly, so instead Demott found work as the stunt rider for actors Mae Marsh—in a movie about a circus rider—and Mabel Normand.[115]

By 1913, Demott was giving lessons in posture and fitness. Clad in black knickers and sweaters, she invited clients to her Long Island estate amid a welter of Pomeranian dogs. You should spend the day wearing riding or exercise gear, she said. "There shall be no display of clothes."[116] Demott wrote a book called *The Circus Lady*, and at seventy-five, she did shoulder stands on a horse in front of an audience.[117] Her hair was white by then, and she took to attending the circus, waving to riders she knew.[118] Like the others, she could not stay away.

Circus riders were, of course, extreme riders, with their rings of fire and athletic, perilous acts. Other women riders' performances and accomplishments overlapped with theirs, as they—diving horse riders, long-distance riders—also sought to outdo each other, and themselves, on horseback.

7

Extreme Riding
The Girls Who Dared

American women like to ride long distances, even when they don't have to. In 2005, Linda Losey rode horseback from Baltimore to California. Losey's son, Sam, died at the age of ten, and the two had long talked about such a trek. She rode in his memory, a pack horse by her side.[1] In *Ride of Her Life*, horsewoman Elizabeth Letts writes about the journey of Annie Wilkins, a Mainer who rode across the country in the 1950s to fulfill her last wish.[2]

In the era of the New Woman, long riding grabbed attention. People loved to read about the short-lived Pony Express and followed cowboy races that traversed states as well as long cross-country rides like that of the Abernathy boys, two children who set out for New York from Oklahoma. Distance riding changed from how you'd move between far-off places to a newsworthy sport. Some women set records by simply covering the same ground over and over, while others rode great swaths of territory. It was as if everyone absolutely needed to know how long someone could possibly stay in the saddle. Some did it on a lark, and others as a means to employment—if they could become famous for their long riding, they might use their celebrity to earn a living.

Meanwhile, other women—concerned, too, with earning money— tested the limits of ability by riding down on diving horses instead of across the country. Diving horses flew with women aboard, stretching audiences' imaginative limits as they careened down from diving boards into tanks full of water. How far? And how high? Horsewomen asked and answered.

⁂

Newspapers offered scattered coverage of long-riding horsewomen, both women who needed to ride and those elected to do so. Sarah Burks, who was twenty-two in 1899, rode her father's fifty-mile mail route through the desert in Arizona. Her father, who had become unable to ride the route, ran a livery stable, and sometimes she would accompany riders who had rented his horses.[3] Mrs. James C. Frazer, carrying two guns and riding astride, rode through Cumberland, Maryland, on March 11, on her way to study law at the University of West Virginia, in Morgantown, a story that made the *Washington Post*.[4] In 1883, when one Californian bet another that she and two friends could make it from Los Angeles to Sierra Madre Villa, fifteen miles away, in an hour and forty-five minutes. They did it in an hour and forty-four.[5] In 1916, two distance riders, Esther McKee and Lorde Stockton Reed, her arm in a sling, camped out as they explored the High Sierras on their horses, Congregational Speed and Tommy Carmelita.[6] Slings and guns, a mail route, and mountain exploration: women taking their horses far held readers' interest.

In 1881, a fair in Minneapolis featured a women's long-distance race. In these, riders swapped out different horses to ride for long periods of time and distance. A promoter found eager challengers to one of the women riders in his show. "I promised Mr. Jewett," said the promoter, "that the next race we had his daughter might take part in it. Well, along in the spring following there appeared in the Associated Press dispatches a challenge from Belle Cooke, a California lady, to ride a race with any woman for the championship of the United States."[7]

Jewett was twenty, Swedish, and the adopted daughter of a farmer's family in western Minnesota. She'd always had a way with horses, including training young ones, and took care of her father's cattle herds on horseback. Cooke, her challenger, was a Californian who performed at fairs and claimed to be the United States' champion lady rider.[8] Jewett's saddle slipped during the ninth mile of the twenty-mile race and she lost, claiming someone had tampered with her girth. "Miss Jewett is a wild, untamed Minnesota girl and there is a State [*sic*] pride in her achievements," a reporter wrote, describing what was at stake in Jewett's accomplishments.[9]

Born in New York, long-rider Nan Aspinwall moved to Nebraska with her parents as a child. By 1908, she and her husband Frank Gable were performing

126   ASTRIDE

with Buffalo Bill's Wild West troupe in combination with Pawnee Bill's. (Nan worked as a belly dancer in Pawnee Bill's group.)[10] She worked as a trick roper in Buffalo Bill's show—she could rope horses by one, two, three, or four legs, and Cody reputedly called her "the Montana Girl."[11] She set out from San Francisco on horseback in 1910. In her saddlebag, she carried food, water, postcards to sell, and a letter from the mayor of San Francisco to the mayor of New York. Ahead stretched hostile deserts and sparsely populated areas. "It takes nerve to ride horseback all the way from the Pacific Ocean to the Atlantic," wrote one reporter. "It takes a whole lot more nerve if you are a woman."[12]

In Denver, Aspinwall rode into town on her Thoroughbred mare Lady Ellen. She had ridden 2,198 miles and felt spent and gloomy:

> My disposition has undergone a complete change, for I was cheerful when I started on this wretched horseback trip across the continent, but now I carry a perpetual grouch. I went once for seven days without a bed to sleep in, flopping myself down in ditches, on platforms along the railroad, in stalls, and in any place I could find. Talk about Western chivalry—I failed to meet any of it. I came near getting pinched at Mitchell, on the top of the pass. There's where my grouch grew so big I couldn't contain it all, and it overflowed and ran through that little town. I couldn't awaken a soul there, and finally rode through the streets shooting into every window. Men came out with guns, then, and I had to ride hard to get away.[13]

Along the way, many people tried to buy Lady Ellen, but Aspinwall refused. She also didn't let anyone else care for her. She slept wherever she could, from tents to inside a barrel.[14] As Mary Higginbotham notes in her book about Aspinwall, she was not always alone, although reports indicated she was. Instead, Frank sometimes traveled along the route generating publicity before she got to each town. "Presumably to complement her image as an exceptional cowgirl who could perform a man's job yet remain feminine and alluring," writes Higginbotham, "the Montana Girl transformed from a thirty-year-old, married woman who likely grew up in Nebraska and whose mother was still alive, into a twenty-four-year-old, unmarried woman who had been born and raised on a prominent Montana ranch, and whose parents were both deceased."[15] As Aspinwall traveled eastward, years fell away and

Aspinwall. (Library of Congress, LCCN 2014686045)

128   ASTRIDE

her story grew. If Frank was identified at all, it was as "advance man" or even as her "brother."

In the desert that stretched from Fallon to Austin, Nevada, Aspinwall rode through herds of feral horses and passed skeletons of people who'd died from heat, cold, or arsenic-tainted water. She bought horse feed from cattle rustlers. On a granite mountain prospecting road, she couldn't find a single trail or hoofprint to guide her back. Exhausted and disoriented, she climbed a nearby peak, only to realize when she got down that the underbrush was so thick that she couldn't see her horse. Then, Aspinwall said, Lady Ellen neighed. Aspinwall believed that sound saved her life.[16] On the descent, the horse cropped some spare grass, but Aspinwall went hungry. They were lost for two days and a night, then found a railroad camp at Proctor.[17] By then, Aspinwall's feet were bare, bloody, and full of thorns. Some railroad men carried her into their camp, and, as Aspinwall told the story, she stayed at the camp for three days, cooking for the group. Next was the Great Salt Lake Desert, which took seven days, and it wasn't until she hit Green River that she found the Denver and Rio Grande Railroad to follow. A bridge washed out, and the water was so high, horse and rider were almost swept away as they swam.[18]

By July 6, Aspinwall had been riding for 178 days. She was in Elizabeth, New Jersey, wretched from heat and mosquitoes.[19] Two days later, she rode into City Hall Square wearing a short khaki skirt and a red shirt. Her face was tanned, and she'd lost more than twenty pounds.[20] She dismounted to hand the letter from San Francisco mayor McCarthy to New York mayor Gaynor's secretary since Gaynor was away.[21] Borough president George McAneney read the letter as about a thousand people gathered in the wake of a cowgirl riding up to the City Hall steps. "I'd rather ride through the wild West than through Broadway," she said, "My little mare was terribly frightened by your elevated trains." She asked reporters for a hotel with a barn attached.[22]

At least one editor reacted with hostility to Aspinwall's press release. "Well, now, really Nancy Jane," ran an editorial in the Leavenworth, Kansas paper, "the Times must decline to get excited over this event." The piece continued:

And then, Nan, the Times really isn't greatly interested in freaks. The man who walks across the continent on a wager, the man who eats five dozen pigs feet at a sitting, the woman who eats a quail every day for thirty days or the woman who bites through sixteen pies is not anything like as interesting to us as the man who stays at home and helps build up his community or the woman who takes care of a home and adds to the population a half dozen good and robust children, or faced by the necessity of earning a living, buckles down to it and does something that is really useful. So you will excuse us Nancy, if we don't get excited over the fact that you have ridden a horse across the continent.[23]

The editor's distaste for Aspinwall's quest, describing her as a "freak," and then suggesting she should stay home raising children, reveals the stakes for extreme horsewomen. Of course, Aspinwall sought fame; she was a performer. Her ability to complete the ride was tied to her livelihood. She needed to ride. Contorting that desire into the same drive that impelled others to eat quail for a month reveals repulsion for Aspinwall's ambition. In the eyes of the Leavenworth editor, Aspinwall was unnatural.

Aspinwall wound up with a bad case of poison ivy and had to rest in Allentown, Pennsylvania.[24] Back home in Montana, she spoke frankly in interviews, saying she'd had enough horseback riding to last her the rest of her life. "I'll never do it again," she told a reporter in Butte, "and I would advise no man or woman to undertake the trip."[25] She and her husband went on to remain in show business as vaudevillians. As for Lady Ellen, she was still famous enough in 1914 that a Bridgewater, New Jersey, newspaper article claimed her as a local.[26]

Situated in open land crisscrossed with Genessee River tributaries, Martha Blow Wadsworth's home, Ashantee, stood in an upstate New York foxhunting mecca.[27] Wadsworth and her husband spent winters in Washington, DC, enjoying the company of friends including Alice Roosevelt Longworth and Ethel Roosevelt.[28] "I think she was one of the most extraordinarily vital persons I have ever met," Lida Fleitmann Bloodgood—who certainly knew her way around vitality—wrote. "Tall, florid, tirelessly energetic, as cultured as she was sporting, until the end of her days she eschewed all comforts and slept with Spartan fortitude the year round on an open veranda—the snows of winter blowing into her hair."[29]

This life force took Wadsworth on some very long horseback rides. In 1907, she rode with friends from Washington the eight hundred miles to

Martha Blow Wadsworth in front of Ashantee. (Courtesy Wadsworth Family Papers, Milne Library, State University of New York at Geneseo, digital collection, MBW C1D3B2 p39d)

Avon.[30] All of the horses were hers, but only Wadsworth and a friend would ride the whole way.[31] Riders stayed with families or at hotels, had picnics, and took the long way if it looked appealing. Luggage and dogs went ahead by car and train.[32] In 1912 she rode from DC to Hot Springs, Virginia, and then to Ashantee. The group camped by the road, cooked their own meals, and sometimes stayed in farmhouses.[33] Helen Taft, the then-president's daughter, rode with Wadsworth for ten days of the month-long trip.[34]

Wadsworth decided to beat Theodore Roosevelt's distance riding accomplishment of 120 miles a day in the officers' training ride, when he'd demanded they ride ninety miles in three days. In January 1909, his last year in office, Roosevelt stayed on horseback from 3:40 a.m. to 8:30 p.m., covering ninety-eight miles of Virginia roads and changing horses twice.

That June, Wadsworth beat that record in a sidesaddle. She mounted at four o'clock in the morning and started circling the valley around her house. By one o'clock the next morning, Wadsworth had ridden 159 miles in sixteen hours, using eight horses and riding in relays, 212 miles in fifteen hours and seven minutes.[35]

Extreme Riding   131

Martha Blow Wadsworth. (Courtesy Wadsworth Family Papers, Milne Library, State University of New York at Geneseo, digital collection, MBW C1D3B2 p40d)

That broke all records for women and matched the men's. The next time, Wadsworth used fourteen horses, clocking about four-minute miles. She didn't eat during the ride and just drank a little bit of water. On the last lap, a doctor checked her, just like a veterinarian checked horses involved in these stunts.[36] "Compared with this remarkable feat President's Roosevelt's famous ride of ninety-eight miles in fourteen hours pales into insignificance. . . . There is absolutely no record of any woman having ever accomplished anything in the way of a ride that at all approximated Mrs. Wadsworth's performance," reported the *Evening Star*.[37]

Wadsworth continued to push her horseback endurance on a 250-mile ride in the Arizona desert, still sidesaddle.[38] She rode along with Marion Oliver, daughter of Assistant Secretary of War Robert Shaw Oliver. Oliver led troopers on a practice endurance ride from Ft. Wingate, New Mexico, to the Grand Canyon. The women riders camped in tents, while the men slept out, doing about thirty-eight miles each day. "It was bully," said Oliver, using Roosevelt's favorite adjective, "and I wish I could take the ride over again."[39]

132   ASTRIDE

Foxhunter May Howard also rode one of Roosevelt's riding tests in 1909, riding ninety-eight miles in fifteen and a half hours and soothing stunned officers' egos by saying she'd loved riding her whole life.[40] She rode astride, wearing a skirted coat over breeches. "I am inclined to think that the trouserettes would look freakish and excite much criticism, so I shall cling to the regulation costume of today, and even though other horsewomen may possibly adopt the trouserettes and short skirts I feel perfectly at home in my riding habit and I ride side saddle [*sic*], too," she said.[41]

In September of 1911 Alberta Claire, who called herself "The Girl from Wyoming," perhaps an allusion to Aspinwall's "Montana Girl" nickname, left Santa Monica in a ceremony at which the mayor spoke, and a band played. She had 110 days to make the trip and would win $1,000 if she made it.[42] She would get to Times Square at noon on June 29, 1912. The trip was more than 8,100 miles. "To prove that Miss Claire has actually ridden all the way, her press agent offers signed statements of the railroad station agents in every town. . . . The entire trip has been made on one horse, and she had pictures people had taken along the way." She took her big dog, Bud with her, although when she rode across Death Valley, she had him shipped ahead by train, because she couldn't carry enough water for him, herself, and Mickey. Her longest ride was from Youngstown, Ohio, to Pittsburgh, which is seventy-three miles. It took her nine hours and fifteen minutes.[43] They rode into the surf at Atlantic City, and Theodore Roosevelt greeted her in Buffalo.[44]

Mostly, people were kind. She rode along with some cowboys, and then made camp with some others, who watered her horse and gave her food. Some said they'd thought she would take the train. "How foolish," she said, "don't you know I'm making this trip because I want to, I love the out-of-doors, and every minute of it interests me?"[45] But, Claire reported, she did stay in one unfriendly town, where she didn't feel safe until a woman offered her dinner and a place to stay. Claire had cast her fifth ballot before she headed out and she wanted to be back in Wyoming in time to vote for president. "She is an enthusiastic, but not militant, suffragist," the *Washington Post* noted.[46]

The inimitable Peek and Marantette sisters counted distance riding as one of their accomplishments. In September of 1883, at Charter Oak racetrack, "Myrtle Peek defeated Madame Marantella [*sic*] in a ten-mile running race, changing horses at each mile; time, 22:04½." Later in the month found them

Alberta Claire, 1913. (Courtesy Champaign County Historical Society photograph collection)

134   ASTRIDE

in Boston. "A 10-mile race for $1,000, a fresh horse to be used at the end of each mile, between Mme. Marantette and Myrtle Peek, was won by the former in 20:40¼."

Of course, Peek and Marantette rode in the circus, as detailed in chapter 6. But they began with the distance feats that were popular at state fairs of the time, and at fourteen, Peek rode twenty miles against time in 43 minutes and 29½ seconds. She'd won a ten-mile race on July 4, splashing through mud. "Sporting men here who saw several of her horses drop from a run into a mere canter after they had been mounted for the third time in the race say that the time made was very remarkable."[47] The next week, there was a ten-mile race at Santa Clara's fair in California between two riders, each of whom used five horses.[48] In 1883, at the driving park in Erie, Pennsylvania, Peek was thrown and rendered unconscious during the eighth mile of a race with her sister. She was just sixteen.[49]

Years later, a reporter asked Marantette if she ever lost her nerve, amid all of this high jumping and distance riding. No, she said, but she admitted that "when I was riding the long races without stopping, changing at every mile, I used to look around the ring when I went in and wonder if I should come off alive."[50]

In extreme endurance riding, women endangered themselves more than their horses. In the diving horse acts popular during the New Woman era, however, audiences feared just as much for the horses, who climbed tall platforms and plummeted to water below. The fall was usually forty feet long, and the tank was about twelve feet deep. Like some sort of conflation of Pegasus and the horses Poseidon mythologically formed into waves, the diving horses went from air to water, transforming from land to air to sea animals mid-harrowing trip.

It could be a violent business. Diving horse rider Sonora Carver's retinas detached after so many forceful plunges into the water, and she went blind in 1923. (Doctors couldn't yet repair that injury as they can today.) She kept riding diving horses until 1934. (Her autobiography, *A Girl and Five Brave Horses*, was the basis for the 1991 movie *Wild Hearts Can't Be Broken*.) Carver's diving horse world, centered around the Atlantic City pier, began toward the end of the New Woman era. But diving horses had existed even earlier.

One of the first acts, G. F. Holloway's, used riderless horses.[51] One article reported that they could jump about fifteen feet down.[52] At Coney Island,

King, 1905. (Library of Congress, LCCN 93513994)

crowds packed in, and shows sold out early in the day. A Kinetoscope image of the horses jumping also became very famous. Holloway told audiences and reporters the following origin story: his horses, named King and Queen, were pastured across a river and high bluff from their mothers. One morning Holloway found the young horses with their dams in the lower pasture. He watched one night and saw them make the leap. He started training them for their act right away.[53] They never had shoes or were broke to saddle.[54] The whole story made the horses' decision to jump seem natural, as if they were born to be mid-air or splashing into the water.

Iowa newspapers debunked the legend Holloway told but said that Holloway did truly see the horses jump first from the banks of an Iowa river, near Bancroft. True also that neighbors scoffed while Holloway's wife encouraged him to keep working with the horses. Viewers liked that Holloway didn't use whips, even to guide the horses, who simply walked up the steps. Holloway felt so confident that the horses would make their jumps without encouragement that he offered a hundred dollars to anyone who bet against him.[55] They performed in England and all over the United States; in Washington, DC, locals could take an excursion boat to see them dive along the Potomac River. Workers dug a tank that was twelve feet deep, twenty feet wide, and thirty feet long.[56] The plunge was forty feet.[57] Humane officers investigated Holloway's act—could the horses really be all right doing this? Strangely, they seemed fine.[58]

Another diving horse trainer, William Frank "Doc" Carver, said he'd gotten the idea for diving horses when some pranksters pulled boards off a bridge so that his horse would fall in the water. Given that he is billed alongside Holloway's diving horses earlier in the century, this seems a little questionable. But the story has something in common with Holloway's: the horses would be doing this anyway. And Carver's story—that he himself was on the first plummeting horse, even by accident—demonstrates that it could be done, much like King and Queen supposedly crossing the water to be with their dams. It also adds to the idea that the women had plenty of options.[59]

In time, Carver—white hat set at a rakish angle, flowing black mustache—owned five diving horses. There was Old Powder Face, not to be confused with Little Powder Face, the smallest horse, who would dive eighty-five feet; Cupid, who "raced" with Old Powder Face as they dived; Silver King, who had a very forward leap; and the Clown Horse.[60] Carver maintained the

Extreme Riding 137

Holloway legacy of whipless performance. "Trained with Sugar and Kindness. Treated as Companions and Friends," ran one of his advertisements. "The diving horses are so highly educated that they are willing to dive from a platform from forty to one hundred feet in height, risking their lives because they love their master."

This is where the women came in. Carver's diving horses were mounted. One rider was the girl in red, the "bravest girl in the world," in "the dip of death," a "wild plunge of forty feet on the back of a high-diving horse, the most startling, sensational, hair-raising, death, defying leap for life."[61]

A reporter in Houston in 1907 watched as a young woman clambered to the top of a forty-foot-high platform and kissed her hand to the audience. Next, an untacked bay horse joined her, held by a groom as the girl mounted astride, grabbing mane. "Nothing stands between her and serious accident and perhaps death but the intelligence of the well-trained horse and her great ability as a horsewoman," the reporter noted, also pointing out that the audience seemed concerned for her safety. Peril produced the spectacle. Carver had found a way to monetize the fascination with the danger inherent in women riding horses.

At a signal, the horse leaped off the platform. The audience sat "still as death, until the horse appears swimming and on its back the smiling white face of the Girl in Red. Then reaction takes place, and the audience simply makes the earth ring with their cheers and congratulations," the article said. Startling and beautiful: the diving horse act was almost surreal, painterly, a scene filled with impossibility. If the balloon horse at the circus hinted at Pegasus-in-flight, then the diving horses embodied him.[62]

Meanwhile, who was this Girl in Red? Advertisements called her the bravest girl in the world, and her act the "most dangerous, daring, nervy, hair-raising, death-defying, flirting-with-eternity act ever placed before the public. She shakes hands with death and smiles at danger."[63] Like the stories surrounding Nan Aspinwall, those around the horses' riders were sometimes wreathed in fancy. In 1906, a woman named Lorena Davis walked into a New Mexico newspaper office and asked where she might find Dr. Carver, because he had offered a hundred-dollar reward to anyone who was game to ride his diving horse Silver King in a forty-foot dive at Traction Park. She was a Californian broncobuster, she said, and had traveled to Albuquerque from Oakland. She was as good as cowgirl Lucille Mulhall at riding untamed horses. "I have come to Albuquerque for the express purpose of riding the

A diving horse and rider, 1905. (Library of Congress, LCCN 2012645715)

horse that Mr. Carver advertised and getting his $100," she said.[64] Whether this Lorena was truly unknown is unclear; in her memoir about her own life as a diving horse rider, Sonora Carver writes that Lorena was also the name of Dr. Carver's granddaughter.[65]

In 1906 at the Agricultural Park in Los Angeles, California, Carver issued a similar challenge. Originally, a jockey and a St. Vincent's college football player said they'd ride, but they vanished at showtime. But a horsewoman was game. As she prepared to ride Cupid in his plunge, she chomped a piece of gum and didn't stop until the dive was complete. "Oh, it was easy," she said. "I have never ridden a horse in just this particular way before, and the one that came down before Cupid did seem to go almost perpendicular in the air."[66]

The diving horses went to the Dreamland amusement park on Coney Island in 1908. A rider named Mamie Francis dived on horseback, using an electric tower as a diving board, fifty feet above the boardwalk.[67] Sonora

Carver's sister, Arnette French, recalled her riding days: "The horse would go down to the bottom and then push himself up,'" she told a reporter in 1985. "'But if a horse turned in the air and didn't land right, he would flounder, and you had to push him up yourself. If you fell off, you had to do the best you could. Otherwise you came out of the tank, took your bow, gave the horse some sugar and that was it.'" If the horse took a straight-down nosedive, the rider "caught the force of the water," the move that damaged Carver's eye.[68]

Sonora Carver was twenty years old in 1923 when a date took her to a county fair. She looked up at a white tower that stretched into the air. She saw a girl wearing a brown football helmet and a red bathing suit sitting on top. At a signal, a dapple-gray mare galloped up a ramp to her, and as the horse swept by, the girl in the red bathing suit slid onto her back. "After looking the crowd over to her satisfaction, she slid her forefeet down. A series of planks, set one beside the other, was nailed flat to the front of the platform, and it was here she braced herself. She hung for a moment at an almost perpendicular angle, then pushed away from the boards and plunged outward into space. For a split second her form was imprinted on the night sky like a silhouette, then her beautiful body arched gracefully over and down and plunged into the tank."[69]

Carver's mother had seen an advertisement Carver had placed for a woman who could swim and dive.[70] At first, Carver laughed. But after the fair, when she thought of that gray mare, she changed her mind. "The fact was that I had fallen in love, simply and completely," she wrote.[71] She signed on.

How did it feel to ride a diving horse? "I felt his muscles tense as his body sprang out and down, and then had an entirely new feeling," writes Carver. "It was a wild, almost primitive feeling that only comes with complete freedom of contact with the earth."[72]

In 1909, the Pittsburgh Hippodrome featured Mamie Francis and her gray horses, Zeda and Kirkland.[73] The show went like this: Kirkland, with little covers over her ears, went first up the thirty-five-foot ramp, and dived alone into the fourteen-foot-deep tank. Next, Francis and Zeda dived together. "It is an awful thrill for spectators," a reporter wrote. "What must it be for the horse and rider?" In reply, Francis, a Westerner whose most memorable childhood toy had been a tin horse, gave a long talk to a reporter.

> The very thrill of [riding diving horses] is a delicious sensation. I don't believe I can describe it. When the horse stands on that platform 50

or 60 feet above the heads of the spectators and I look down into the vista of faces before me, there is no realization of impending danger. I can feel the horse pulsating with emotion as I sit astride him. I can feel his heart beat with mine. I know that he is enjoying the same thrill that I do, and when he jumps, oh, the glory of it. I just close my eyes, take a deep breath and await the splash in the tank below. There is no thud, no jar. It is just such a jump as I might take on my horse over a six-rail fence. Am I not afraid? If I were I would not do it. Some time, they tell me, I will surely be dashed to pieces, but I am too much of a fatalist to worry about little things like that.[74]

In October of 1922, a diving horse act at the interstate fair in Chattanooga, Tennessee, received attention not because of audience excitement, but because a humane society saw violations. Apparently, during one performance, the horse did not want to make the leap. "He did not jump," an onlooker said, "he fell, and with him the girl. She clung to him, hanging to his neck, white and awful looking. The horse made the bank—he jumped forty-seven feet, landing in water." Afterward, the rider couldn't walk, so attendants helped her leave the area. The crowd went from cheery fairgoers to outraged activists, with the girl deemed as much in need of rescue as the horse. "Every woman there almost knows the girl didn't want to do it—and the horse! Oh, that horse will never let me forget him," said a local activist.[75] Onlookers called the Humane Society the next day. The spectacle had soured.

Whether riding great distances across open country or dropping into water seemingly from the sky, extreme riders pushed natural limits, molding the world around them into a place to display their extraordinary experiences. The extreme riders embraced danger as publicly as circus riders, in a way that demanded witnessing, whether from audiences in bleachers or simply from their horses themselves.

As the reporter who interviewed diving rider Mamie Francis noted, "The girl spoke with evident sincerity. There was nothing of vain glory [sic] in her tones. Nothing of boastfulness. It was a plain frank statement from a girl who dares."

Epilogue

I drove to the National Sporting Library in Middleburg, Virginia, to work one misty fall afternoon. It's one of my favorite places, filled with equestrian books and paintings, and entirely suitable in a horse-obsessed area of the country. But I hadn't checked before leaving home, and the library was closed for a polo classic taking place nearby. I was sorry to miss my time there, but I had to admit I appreciated the idea of a library that closed for a horse event.

So, I spread my jacket on a bench and settled outside with my laptop, near a statue of the 1993 Kentucky Derby winner Sea Hero that I like. The sculptor, Tessa Pullan, captured him walking and looking forward with perked ears and a friendly, interactive expression—the Thoroughbred's regal bearing tempered with horsey curiosity and kindness, the kind of demeanor I think I see in my part-Thoroughbred mare, Audie, when she's at her most engaging.

This day, though, I noticed another sculpture, not as large. It is of a woman and horse, on opposite ends of a balance beam, each with a foot off the ground. The horse, the proportions of a draft cross or old-school rosinback, is muscled, and his neck is arched, mouth open in concentration, tail (the suggestion of a braid evoking an audience nearby) to the side as he works. Across from him, the woman stands on one foot with her arms upraised, in a dress reminiscent of a circus performer's. She is muscled, too, like the horse, and both have big eyes and studied gazes. These two are fixed in work and play, evidence of practice in the physical joyfulness and grace of their positions. Although the horse and woman are not staring at each other, their motion harmonizes. It's powerful, a couple of beings, both prepared to

A girl feeds a horse some oats, 1903. (Library of Congress, LCCN 90715440)

spring into further action. Standing by the sculpture, eyes about level with the beam, I could feel the command of each, and the tension provided by their unity.

The name of the sculpture, which is by Diana Reuter-Twining, is "Equipoise," an appropriate name for a modern sculpture that's also a timeless image. Its strength harked back to the pull of the women in this book, many of whom I researched at this library.

A twentieth- and twenty-first-century experience on horseback ties me—and, I'm hoping, readers—to those women, and foregrounds the timeless quality of a life lived with horses. Listening to pastured horses cropping grass, slipping a headstall over patient ears, adjusting a stirrup from the saddle—these familiar equestrian gestures span years.

The American women riders of the 1890–1920 era quested for societal equipoise as they worked, played, and lived with animals. Ever-ready, like the two figures in Reuter-Twining's sculpture, the horsewomen understood horses as partners in their changing world. They may not have yet comprehended what the new time would bring. But they knew they'd be able to ride through it.

And they knew they wouldn't be alone.

Acknowledgments

I owe a great debt to the many people who helped me with the planning, researching, and writing of *Astride*. The John H. Daniels Fellowship I received from the National Sporting Library helped me sharpen the book's focus, understand the breadth of the material, and allowed me to work (and live) at the home of one of the most special collections around.

I want to thank Patrick O'Dowd, formerly at the University Press of Kentucky, for all his patience, time, and effort. I have been very lucky to work with him, Margaret Kelly, and Jamie Nicholson, series editor of the Horses in History series. The press's readers offered helpful comments along the way. Jennifer Collins copyedited with thoroughness and valuable ideas, and Gayathri Umashankaran attentively oversaw production. I am a longtime admirer of Katherine C. Mooney's excellent and important work and grateful to her for writing the foreword.

I also appreciate the attention of Elizabeth Argentieri at the State University of New York at Geneseo, Sherrie Bowser at the Champaign County Historical Archives, and Kelly Coffman, Roda Ferraro, and Becky Ryder at the Keeneland Library.

My writers' group—Joel Achenbach, Matthew Davis, Juliet Eilperin, David Grinspoon, Josh Horwitz, Jacki Lyden, Eric Weiner, and Florence Williams—spent a lot of time listening to horsewomen stories and helped me imagine the book's structure and tone. A particular thank-you to Josh Pons for his time and for allowing me access to some of the most interesting material around. Many thanks as well to Sarah Blake, Anne Dickerson, Nate DiMeo, Joe Heyman, Anne Kornblut, Kitson Jazynka, Tracey Madigan, Margaret McEvoy, Lauri Menditto, Paula O'Rourke, and Christy Ross.

I truly appreciate my whole family, who has supported this long endeavor, and offer a special thank-you to Adam McGraw.

Notes

Foreword

1. Alastair Down, "To See a Woman Win the Grand National Is One of the Greatest Joys of My Life," *Racing Post*, April 11, 2021, https://www.racingpost.com/news/festivals/grand-national-festival/to-see-a-woman-win-the-grand-national-is-one-of-the-greatest-joys-of-my-life-a1gnB6B3x5K9/.

2. Chris Cook, "How Eddie O'Leary's Taxi Journey Set Rachael Blackmore on the Path to Greatness," *Racing Post*, March 18, 2022, https://www.racingpost.com/news/reports/the-taxi-journey-that-opened-up-rachael-blackmores-path-to-superstar-status-aU18J8Z9n9Cr/.

3. Richard Forristal, "'She's Got Bigger Balls Than Any of the Boys'—the Making of Rachael Blackmore," *Racing Post*, March 27, 2021, https://www.racingpost.com/news/features/shes-got-bigger-balls-than-any-of-the-boys-the-making-of-rachael-blackmore-anV6o7N0YBKT/.

4. Lee Mottershead, "Pale, Exhausted and Overcome—But Blackmore Is Also Utterly Brilliant," *Racing Post*, March 18, 2022, https://www.racingpost.com/news/reports/pale-exhausted-overcome-and-utterly-brilliant-blackmore-has-won-the-gold-cup-aNDM94n9dlCQ/.

5. Hollie Doyle, "Hollie the History Maker," interview by Nick Luck, *Nick Lucky Daily*, podcast, episode 509, June 20, 2022.

6. John Randall, "A New High: Doyle Becomes First Female Rider to Land Group 1 Classic in Europe," *Racing Post*, June 19, 2022, https://www.racingpost.com/news/a-new-high-doyle-becomes-first-female-rider-to-land-group-1-classic-in-europe-aQtp20h6KHPV/.

7. Ulrich Raulff, *Farewell to the Horse*, trans. Ruth Ahmedzai Kemp (London: Allen Lane, 2017), 267.

8. Bradwell v. The State of Illinois. 83 U.S. 130 (1873), 141.

9. "100 Victims of Suffrage Parade Are in Hospitals," *Baltimore Evening Sun*, March 4, 1913, 6.

10. Joanna Scutts, *Hotbed: Bohemian Greenwich Village and the Secret Club That Sparked Modern Feminism* (New York: Seal, 2022), 7.

11. "Should Women Attend Races?," Kentucky Live Stock Record, August 18, 1894, 97–98.

12. Kathleen E. McCrone, *Playing the Game: Sport and the Physical Emancipation of English Women, 1870–1914* (Lexington: University Press of Kentucky, 1988), 9.

13. Raulff, *Farewell to the Horse*, 10–11, 229–30.

14. Elizabeth Cady Stanton, *Solitude of Self* (Washington, DC: Government Printing Office, 1915), 1–2.

Preface

1. C. De Hurst, *How Women Should Ride* (New York: Harper & Brothers, 1892), 249.

2. Lara Prior-Palmer, *Rough Magic* (New York: Catapult, 2019), 215.

3. Ulrich Raulff, *Farewell to the Horse*, trans. Ruth Ahmedzai Kemp (New York: Liveright, 2018), 31.

4. "A Life Among Horses," *New York Times*, April 12, 1903, 28.

Prologue

1. "Miss Dorothy Chestick May Ride Astride When She Chooses," *Buffalo Evening News*, September 13, 1895, 5.

2. "A Female Centaur," *Baltimore Sun*, September 3, 1895, 4.

3. "Can Ride Astride," *Muscatine News-Tribune*, October 4, 1895, 6.

4. "May Ride as She Pleases," *San Francisco Chronicle*, September 7, 1895, 9.

5. Adrienne Mayor, *The Amazons* (Princeton: Princeton UP, 2014), 170.

6. Lida Fleitmann Bloodgood, *Saddle of Queens* (London: J. A. Allen, 1959), 42.

7. Elliott Coues, "Riding Both Sides," *Harrisburg Telegraph*, February 18, 1896, 3.

8. Elizabeth Dudley, "Riding Man-Fashion," *Chicago Tribune*, August 22, 1872, 6.

9. "Riding Clothes-Pin Fashion," *Des Moines Register*, January 5, 1873, 2.

10. "Cross-Wise Riding," *Washington Evening Star*, May 18, 1895, 15.

11. "Shall Woman Ride Astride?," *St. Louis Post-Dispatch*, March 17, 1895, 31.

12. "Bestride Their Steeds Like Men," *Chicago Tribune*, November 4, 1895, 1.

13. "Discards Skirts on Horseback," *Chicago Daily Tribune*, September 5, 1896, 13.

14. Cornelia A. Little, "Ladies Riding Astride," *The Country Gentleman*, October 8, 1863, 22.

15. "Ride Astride? No, Say U.C.V.," *Asheville Gazette-News*, May 26, 1913, 1.

16. "Women Ride Astride," *Chicago Tribune*, March 22, 1890, 9.

Notes to Pages 6–15   147

17. "Women Ride Astride," 9.

18. "Women Ride Astride," 9.

19. "Miss Jenness Rides Like a Man," *Washington Post*, March 23, 1890, 10.

20. Laura Giddings, "The Lady Who Rides Astride," *Wichita Daily Eagle*, April 16, 1890, 7.

21. "Shall Modern Horsewomen Go Back to the Sidesaddle?," *New York Sun*, October 8, 1911, L4.

22. "Crime for Women to Ride Astride," *Chicago Daily Tribune*, July 28, 1909, 3.

23. "His Modesty Was Shocked," *Charlotte Observer*, July 27, 1909, 1.

24. "Crime for Women to Ride Astride," *Chicago Daily Tribune*, July 28, 1909, 3.

25. "Astride Barred," *Los Angeles Times*, May 29, 1913, 11.

26. "Throws, Kills, Girl Rider," *Los Angeles Times*, July 6, 1909, III 1.

27. "Girl Dragged by a Stirrup," *New York Times*, August 5, 1896, 1.

28. "Furious Horse Slays Woman," *Atlanta Constitution*, May 14, 1904, 1.

29. "Woman, 24, Killed in Fall from Horse Had Borrowed," *Washington Post*, May 14, 1932.

30. "Women Ride Astride," 9.

31. "Horse 'Diabolo' Kills Girl Rider," *Chicago Daily Tribune*, May 26, 1911, 1.

32. "Young Horsewoman Killed," *New York Sun*, August 1, 1900, 1.

33. "Ride Astride? Sure," *Indiana Gazette*, May 29, 1913, 1.

1. Riding for the Vote

1. "Expect More Trouble Today," *Boston Globe*, June 6, 1913, 16.

2. Discord, "Female Suffrage," *Colman's Rural World*, May 29, 1969, 22, 346.

3. Mary Chapman, "Women and Masquerade in the 1913 Suffrage Demonstration in Washington," *American Studies* 44, no. 3, Body/Art (1999): 349.

4. Jill Lepore, *The Secret History of Wonder Woman* (New York: Vintage, 2015), 21.

5. Alison Piepmeier, *Out in Public* (Chapel Hill: North Carolina UP, 2004), 5.

6. Lumsden, Linda J., *Inez: The Life and Times of Inez J. Milholland* (Bloomington: Indiana UP, 2004), 6.

7. Holly J. McCammon, "'Out of the Parlors and into the Streets,'" *Social Forces* 81, no. 3 (March 2003); 795.

8. Lepore, *Secret History of Wonder Woman*, 16.

9. "To Ride in Pageant," *Washington Evening Star*, January 10, 1913, 3.

10. "Rival Beauties Are Matched," *Chicago Examiner*, January 23, 1913, 9.

11. Lumsden, *Inez*, 87.

12. "Promise to Speed the Suffrage Bill," *New York Times*, March 13, 1912, 3.

13. "In Saddle for Votes," *Washington Post*, February 11, 1912, 8.

14. "In Saddle," 8.

15. "Suffrage Army Out on Parade," *New York Times*, May 5, 1912, 1.

16. "Suffrage Army," 1.

148   Notes to Pages 15–23

17. "Suffrage Army," 1.

18. "Suffrage Army," 1.

19. "Suffrage Army," 1.

20. Frank I. Whitehead, "In March for Votes," *Washington Post*, January 28, 1912, 5.

21. Whitehead, "In March," 5.

22. "March Like Men," *Baltimore Sun*, June 29, 1912, 20.

23. Whitehead, "In March," 5.

24. The Roosevelts had a horse named Grey Dawn. I have to wonder if it was the same horse, but I have not been able to definitely find out.

25. Chapman, "Women and Masquerade," 349.

26. "Women March Today," *Washington Post*, February 12, 1913, 5.

27. "To Join 10,000 Sisters," *Baltimore Sun*, January 11, 1913, 3; "Horsewomen in Parade," *New York Times*, January 11, 1913, 6.

28. "Welcoming Army Meets Militants," *Ogden (UT) Standard*, February 26, 1913, 3.

29. "To Join 10,000 Sisters," *Baltimore Sun*, January 11, 1913, 3.

30. "Horsewomen in Parade," 6; "Mrs. Longworth to Ride in 'Petticoat Cavalry,'" *Leavenworth (KS) Times*, January 18, 1913, 2.

31. "Inez Milholland," accessed April 22, 2024, https://www.nps.gov/people/inez-milholland.htm.

32. Lumsden, *Inez*, 84.

33. Lumsden, *Inez*, 84.

34. "To Ride in Pageant," *Washington Evening Star*, January 10, 1913, 3.

35. National Park Service, "Gateway Arch and Lady Liberty's Original Torch Go Purple and Gold for Women's Suffrage," https://www.nps.gov/orgs/1207/19th-amendment-forward-into-light.htm. Accessed July 19, 2024.

36. "Women Play Big Part in Wilson's Inauguration," *Princeton (MN) Union*, February 20, 1913, 2.

37. "Men Are to March," *Manchester Democrat-Radio*, March 5, 1913, 3.

38. "5,000 Women in Suffrage Parade," *Baltimore Sun*, March 4, 1913, 2.

39. National Park Service, "1913 Woman Suffrage Procession," https://www.nps.gov/articles/woman-suffrage-procession1913.htm. Accessed July 19, 2024.

40. "Inez Milholland," photograph, *Baltimore Sun*, March 4, 1913, 2.

41. "Jeers and Insulting Remarks for Women in Suffrage Parade," *Hutchinson Daily*, March 4, 1913, n.p.

42. "Jeers and Insulting Remarks," n.p.

43. "Pick Mrs. Kayser to Lead Brigade," *Chicago Daily Tribune*, April 15, 1914, 9.

44. "Mrs. K. Fairbank to Ride at Head of Suffragists," *Chicago Daily Tribune*, March 27, 1914, 15.

45. "Horsewomen Out to Practice for Suffrage Parade," *Chicago Daily Tribune*, April 17, 1914, 13.

46. "Division for Babies in Suffrage Parade," *New York Times*, October 22, 1915, 20.

Notes to Pages 24–29   149

2. Urban Riding, Horse Shows, and Foxhunting

1. "Accomplished Belles," *Washington Post*, September 1, 1889, 9; "Some Ladies Who Ride," *Washington Post*, February 17, 1889, 14.

2. "Horse-Riding in Central Park," *New York Times*, June 8, 1871, 4.

3. "'Beauty Riding' as a Fad," *Chicago Daily Tribune*, November 21, 1909, 14.

4. "Gotham Tales," *Fort Worth Daily Gazette*, April 20, 1890, 10.

5. "Horse-Back Riders," *Washington Post*, December 22, 1889, 17; "At Ease in the Saddle," *Washington Post*, February 21, 1892, 10; "Horse-Back Riders," 17.

6. "About Us," accessed February 13, 2023, https://manhattansaddlery.com/pages/about-us.

7. "In the Metropolis," *Virginia (MN) Enterprise*, May 5, 1905, 2.

8. "Girl on Horseback Stops a Runaway," *New York Times*, June 11, 1910, 2.

9. "Agnes Miller a Horsewoman," *New York Times*, March 8, 1896, 10.

10. "A Lady's Ride on a Runaway Horse," *New York Times*, November 30, 1883, 8.

11. "Shopping on Horseback," *Illustrated Police News*, May 12, 1900, 3.

12. "Beat the Wheel," *Illustrated Police News*, October 12, 1895, 2.

13. "Beauty A-Horseback," *Daily American* (Nashville), May 11, 1890, n.p.

14. "How a Girl Won the Prize at a Paper Chase," *Chicago Daily Tribune*, December 19, 1891, 16.

15. "From a Horse's Back," *Chicago Daily Tribune*, August 27, 1893, 27; "Women Who Can Drive," *Chicago Tribune*, August 15, 1897, 38.

16. "Devotees of the Saddle," *New York Times*, December 4, 1898, 20.

17. "Devotees of the Saddle," 20.

18. "Horse-Back Riders," 17.

19. "Horsewomen in Fine Form," *New York Sun*, February 20, 1910, 3.

20. "The Code among Riding Women Is Severity and Smartness," *Vogue*, November 1, 1916, 53.

21. Belle Beach, "Riding Equipment and Care of the Horse," *Vogue*, August 1, 1910, 21–22.

22. "On the Park Bridle-Paths," *Harper's Weekly*, November 12, 1887, 825.

23. "American Horsewomen Noted," *Atlanta Constitution*, June 1, 1902, A3.

24. "Women Who Ride," *Independence (KS) Daily Reporter*, January 30, 1894, 4.

25. "'Beauty Riding' as a Fad," 14.

26. "How to Go Horseback Riding without a Horse," *Chicago Tribune*, July 21, 1907, F2.

27. Mrs. Symes, "How to Be Healthy and Beautiful," *Los Angeles Times*, November 9, 1902, D10.

28. "Woman on Horseback," *The Literary World*, June 12, 1884, 15.

29. "Woman on Horseback," 15.

30. "Women as Horseback Riders," *New York Times*, June 16, 1884, 3.

31. "How the Society Bud Learns Horseback Riding," *Washington Post*, December 30, 1906, E7.

150   Notes to Pages 29–36

32. "How the Society Bud Learns," E7.

33. "Women to Start Coaching Season," *New York Times*, April 28, 1912, C8.

34. "Fun of Riding Indoors," *Baltimore Sun*, January 12, 1903, 9.

35. "'Beauty Riding' as a Fad," 14.

36. "Louisville's Society Girls Turn Their Attention to the Horse," *Louisville Courier-Journal*, November 24, 1901, 19.

37. A Practical Horsewoman, "Women on Horseback," *Harper's Bazaar*, August 2, 1879, 494.

38. A Practical Horsewoman, "Women on Horseback," 494.

39. "How Ladies Should Ride Horseback," *Baltimore Sun*, August 1, 1885, 6.

40. Diana Crossways, "How to Buy a Horse," *Atlanta Constitution*, August 19, 1894, 8.

41. A Practical Horsewoman, "Women on Horseback," 494.

42. "Deserting Bridle Paths," *New York Times*, May 27, 1900, 6; Lida Fleitmann Bloodgood, *Hoofs in the Distance* (New York: Van Nostrand, 1953), 22.

43. Aaron Taylor, "NYC Horse History: Durland's Riding Academy," accessed February 13, 2023, https://manhattansaddlery.com/blogs/news/nyc-horse-history -Durland's-riding-academy.

44. Bloodgood, *Hoofs in the Distance*, 55.

45. Bloodgood, *Hoofs in the Distance*, 22.

46. "Rough-Riding Classes," *New York Times*, February 10, 1895, 6.

47. Bloodgood, *Hoofs in the Distance*, 26.

48. "The President and Mrs. Roosevelt," *Washington Post*, January 28, 1906, 5.

49. "Saves His Daughter," *Baltimore Sun*, July 11, 1902, 8.

50. "Miss Ethel's Riding Habit," *Baltimore Sun*, October 5, 1904, 6.

51. "Whirl of Society," *Topeka Daily Capital*, May 24, 1903, 11.

52. "Ethel Roosevelt's Escape," *Washington Post*, July 16, 1906, 1.

53. "President's Daughter Thrown in Runaway," *New York Times*, September 15, 1906, 1.

54. "Young Roosevelts Can't Ride," *Baltimore Sun*, January 11, 1908, 11.

55. "Ethel Roosevelt in Mishap," *Chicago Daily Tribune*, November 6, 1908, 1.

56. "Girls Angered President," *Baltimore Sun*, December 17, 1908, 1.

57. "Mum on Scolding from President," *Chicago Daily Tribune*, December 19, 1908, 5.

58. "Roosevelt Spares Horse When He Scolds the Girls," *Chicago Daily Tribune*, December 20, 1908, 7.

59. "Denies President Hit Horse," *New York Times*, February 2, 1909, 1.

60. "Thanked by Roosevelt," *New York Times*, February 9, 1909, 1.

61. "Riding Bareback," *Chicago Daily Tribune*, October 21, 1888, 28.

62. "Women Exhibitors Win at Horse Show," *New York Times*, April 28, 1909, 6; "American Has Many Expert Horsewomen," *New York Daily Tribune*, May 31, 1908, 4.

63. "Cheers of Victory Open Horse Show," *New York Times*, November 12, 1918, 16.

Notes to Pages 36–45   151

64. "Vanderbilt a Victor," *New York Daily Tribune*, November 18, 1904, 4.

65. "Atlanta's Social World Is Busy," *Atlanta Constitution*, October 11, 1903, C2.

66. Bloodgood, *Hoofs in the Distance*, 80–81.

67. "Woman Rider Hurt in Jumping Contest," *New York Times*, October 2, 1915, 6.

68. Bloodgood, *Hoofs in the Distance*, 66.

69. "Society Girl Rider, Recently Hurt, at Horse Show in Invalid's Chair," *Washington Post*, November 12, 1915, 6.

70. Bloodgood, *Hoofs in the Distance*, 81.

71. Mary E. Miller, *Baroness of Hobcaw* (Columbia: South Carolina UP, 2006), 53.

72. Helen Ward, "The Riding Woman," *Los Angeles Times*, January 14, 1894, 20.

73. "Famous Horsewoman Coming," *Baltimore Sun*, May 24, 1911, 8.

74. Martha Root, "Interest Grows in Big Show," *Pittsburgh Post*, June 25, 1910, 3.

75. "Woman Jockey Gets Divorce," *Washington Post*, January 31, 1909, 11.

76. "Horse Show a Busy Mart," *New York Sun*, November 16, 1910, n.p.

77. "Big Society Parade at the Horse Show," *New York Times*, November 21, 1911, 3.

78. "Big Society Parade," 3; "Judging Pairs," *New York Tribune*, November 16, 1910, 1.

79. "Horse Show Programme [*sic*]," *Indianapolis Journal*, October 13, 1902, 2.

80. "Cowboy Sport at Idyllwild," *Los Angeles Times*, August 27, 1905, V18.

81. "Champion Horsewoman of America," *San Francisco Call*, December 2, 1900, n.p.

82. "Other Sportsmen Die," *Reading Eagle*, December 27, 1926, 12.

83. Ward, "The Riding Woman," 20.

84. *Horse Show Monthly* 19 (1904).

85. "Miss Beach Criticizes Show," *Chicago Daily Tribune*, November 2, 1900, 5.

86. "Vanderbilt Tandem Lost," *New York Times*, April 8, 1903, 6.

87. "Mrs. Gerken's Big Night," *New York Times*, April 30, 1904.

88. "Show Ring Prize Scorned," *New York Times*, July 31, 1903, 7.

89. "Mrs. Gerken Refuses Award," *New York Times*, July 22, 1906, 5.

90. "Mrs. Gerken's Prize Winners," *New York Times*, May 31, 1902, 6.

91. "Blue Ribbons for Women," *New York Times*, April 7, 1904, 7.

92. "Blue Ribbons," 5.

93. "Eastern Stock Farm Managed by a Woman," *New York Times*, August 30, 1903, 34.

94. "Eastern Stock Farm," 34.

95. Emily Post, *Etiquette in Society, in Business, in Politics and at Home* (New York: Funk & Wagnalls, 1922), 522.

96. "Belle Beach," *Horse Show Monthly* 19 (1904): n.p.

97. Belle Beach, "The Making of a Horsewoman," *Vogue*, February 26, 1910.

98. "Everybody at the Show," *Baltimore Sun*, November 15, 1905, 1.

99. "Champion Horsewoman of America."

100. Belle Beach, "When Miss America Rides," *Atlanta Constitution*, May 7, 1916, A1.

152   Notes to Pages 45–55

101. "Society Outside the Capital," *Washington Post*, March 8, 1911, 7.

102. "Society Outside the Capital," 7; "Mrs. Belle Beach, Horsewoman, Dies," *New York Times*, January 9, 1926, 17.

103. Belle Beach, *Riding and Driving for Women* (New York: Charles Scribner's Sons), 1912, 2.

104. Beach, *Riding and Driving*, 29.

105. Beach, *Riding and Driving*, 101.

106. Beach, *Riding and Driving*, 142.

107. Beach, *Riding and Driving*, 58.

108. "Storage Notices," *New York Tribune*, November 7, n.d., 15.

109. "Belle Beach a Bankrupt," *New York Times*, April 5, 1914, 13.

110. "World's Greatest Horsewoman Dies, Forgotten, in Obscurity," *Rochester Democrat Chronicle*, January 24, 1926, 1.

111. Beach, *Riding and Driving*, vii.

112. "Hunting as a Sport for Women," *Harper's Weekly*, n.d., 1230; "Mrs. Thomas Hitchcock, Jr.," *Saint Paul Globe*, March 6, 1904, 4.

113. Beach, *Riding and Driving*, 58.

114. Belle Beach, "The Making of a Horsewoman," *Vogue*, February 26, 1910.

115. Eleanor Lexington, "Society Dianas," *Los Angeles Times*, November 10, 1895, 28.

116. "When Roosevelt Rode to Hounds," *New York Times*, October 19, 1902, 11.

117. "Following the Pack," *Washington Post*, March 24, 1901, 22.

118. "Horse Is Coming Back into His Kingdom," *Atlanta Constitution*, September 1, 1912, C8B.

3. Women and Humane Societies

1. Susan J. Pearson, *The Rights of the Defenseless* (Chicago: Chicago UP, 2020), 46.

2. Hilary J. Sweeney, "Pasture to Pavement," *American Journal of Irish Studies* 11 (2014): 132.

3. Clay McShane, "Gelded Age Boston," *New England Quarterly* 74, no. 2 (June 2001): 279–80.

4. McShane, "Gelded Age Boston," 285.

5. "Past of the Balloon Horse," *New York Times*, April 4, 1908, 9.

6. "Mr. Roosevelt Friend of the Horse," *Baltimore Sun*, November 14, 1901, 3; "Anecdotes about the New President," *Los Angeles Times*, September 28, 1901, 4.

7. Diane L. Beers, *For the Prevention of Cruelty* (Athens: Ohio UP, 2006), 9–10.

8. McShane, "Gelded Age Boston," 285.

9. McShane, "Gelded Age Boston," 285.

10. Beers, *For the Prevention of Cruelty*, 9–10.

11. "Ill Treating Animals," *New York Tribune*, February 15, 1907, 4.

12. Ann Norton Greene, *Horses at Work* (Cambridge: Harvard UP, 2008), 254.

13. Greene, *Horses at Work*, 254.

Notes to Pages 55–61   153

14. "Editor's Introduction," Mark Twain, *A Horse's Tale*, 1907 (Lincoln: Nebraska UP, 2020), xxi.

15. "Pity the Poor Horse," *Baltimore Sun*, December 26, 1905, 4.

16. "Noble Women Come to Aid the Cause," *Times-Picayune* (New Orleans), February 7, 1896, 6.

17. "Noble Women," 6.

18. Caroline Earle White, "A School for Drivers," *The Times* (Philadelphia), March 22, 1894, 7.

19. "Women in Auto 'Tag' Horses," *Chicago Daily Tribune*, December 16, 1909, 5.

20. "Former Shreveport Woman Becoming National Figure," *Shreveport Times*, August 24, 1914, 3.

21. "Fashion's Cruel Fad," *Washington Post*, January 6, 1897, 7.

22. "Fashion's Cruel Fad," 7.

23. "Mr. Roosevelt Friend of the Horse," 3.

24. "Against Dock-Tail Horses," *New York Times*, December 10, 1901, 8.

25. "County Humane Society," *Knoxville Sentinel*, April 17, 1911, 43.

26. E. H. Packard, "To Stop the Inhuman Crimes against Horses," *Osage City Free Press*, August 28, 1913, 6; "Spreading the Gospel of Kindness to Dumb Beasts," *Bangor Daily News*, March 11, 1913, 2.

27. "Horses Suffer Because of Saloons," *Vogue*, October 25, 1906, 574.

28. "Protects a Fallen Horse," *Chicago Daily Tribune*, December 14, 1899, 13.

29. "A Woman Saves Two Horses from Fire," *New York Times*, January 14, 1896, 15.

30. "Woman Blocks Loop Traffic Fighting Battle of Horse," *Chicago Daily Tribune*, July 13, 1912, 1.

31. "Cruelty to Horses Charged; Woman Accuses Two Men," *Chicago Daily Tribune*, July 21, 1910, 3.

32. "Shoppers Pitied a Horse," *New York Times*, October 6, 1903, 9.

33. "'Nice Little Horse' for $2.50," *Chicago Daily Tribune*, June 20, 1914, 5.

34. "'Helpful Hint' Is Costly," *Chicago Daily Tribune*, November 10, 1904, 1.

35. "Humane Brooklyn Women," *New York Times*, April 21, 1895, 16.

36. "Animals Are Mistreated," *Topeka Daily Capital*, November 27, 1904, 6.

37. "Women Who Are Waging Campaign on Behalf of Unfit Horses," *Chicago Daily Tribune*, March 30, 1903, 4.

38. "Women Who Are Waging Campaign," 4.

39. Laura Lindsay Kerlin, "Brutal Drivers of Horses," *Washington Post*, January 17, 1901, 11; "Pity Fire Engine Horses," *Chicago Daily Tribune*, March 9, 1904, 4.

40. Kerlin, "Brutal Drivers of Horses," 11; "Pleas for Suffering Horse," *Chicago Daily Tribune*, January 21, 1908, 16.

41. "Horses to Have a Minimum Working Day of 12 Hours," *Chicago Daily Tribune*, December 31, 1913, 11.

42. "Gives $25,000 for a Horse Hospital," *New York Times*, January 24, 1912, 10; "Ask Aid for Work Horses," *New York Times*, May 13, 1918, 5; "Gives $25,000 for a Horse Hospital," *New York Times*, January 24, 1912, 10.

43. "Women's League for Animals Exhibit," *New York Times*, February 20, 1913, 11; "Welfare of the Horse," *Evening Times* (Washington, DC), April 16, 1901, 3.

44. Eliza McGraw, "Why Horses Used to Wear Bonnets, Caps, and Peaked Straw Hats," *Washington Post*, August 1, 2017, accessed February 1, 2022 https://www.washingtonpost.com/news/animalia/wp/2017/08/01/why-horses-used-to-wear-bonnets-caps-and-peaked-straw-hats/.

45. "Women to Protect Horses," *New York Times*, July 8, 1904, 9.

46. "Anti-Cruelty Societies' Convention," *New York Times*, October 1, 1900, 7.

47. "Asks Kindness for Horses," *Chicago Daily Tribune*, January 18, 1901, 12.

48. "A Parade for Work Horses," *New York Times*, March 31, 1907, 17.

49. "2,500 Horses Parade on Fifth Avenue," *New York Times*, May 31, 1913, 11.

50. "Say Man's Horse Is Husband Test," *Chicago Daily Tribune*, April 11, 1910, 9.

51. Eliza McGraw, "When Humane Societies Threw Christmas Parties for Horses," *Smithsonian Magazine*, December 17, 2021, accessed February 1, 2022, https://www.smithsonianmag.com/history/when-humane-societies-threw-christmas-parties-for-horses-180979253/.

52. Greene, *Horses at Work*, 252.

53. "Where Horses May Drink," *New York Times*, August 5, 1911, 6.

54. "Friends of the Horse Plan for His Comfort," *Indianapolis News*, October 17, 1912, 22.

55. "72,000 Horses at Work Here," *New York Times*, March 18, 1912, 8.

56. "Rest Cures Here for Poor Horses," *New York Times*, May 30, 1920, 12.

57. "War Horses Scarce," *Pittsburgh Press*, June 24, 1917, 14.

58. "Horrors of Life for Horses in Chicago," *Chicago Daily Tribune*, July 14, 1907, F2.

59. McShane, "Gelded Age Boston," 292–93.

60. Sweeney, "Pasture to Pavement," 142.

61. "Valuable Horse Killed," *New York Times*, March 27, 1900, 7.

62. "Horse Runs into Auto," *Baltimore Sun*, September 18, 1915, 12.

63. "Woman Wins Merciful Death for Aged Horse," *New York Times*, May 14, 1905, 9.

64. "When the Horse Had Colic," *New York Times*, January 21, 1909, 18.

65. "Two Famous Chicago Horsewomen," *Chicago Daily Tribune*, October 19, 1902, A2.

66. "Two Famous Chicago Horsewomen," A2.

67. Lida Fleitmann Bloodgood, *Hoofs in the Distance* (New York: Van Nostrand, 1953), 99.

68. Greene, *Horses at Work*, 54.

4. Women in Racing

1. "Bob Davis Recalls," *Buffalo Evening News*, May 21, 1929, 8.

2. "A Beauty in Jockey Habit," *National Police Gazette*, September 21, 1878, 4.

Notes to Pages 69–74   155

3. Henry Clay Simpson, Jr., *Josephine Clay: Pioneer Horsewoman of the Bluegrass* (Louisville, KY: Harmony House, 2005), 63.

4. "Biography/History," Josephine Russell Erwin Clay papers, University of Kentucky Special Collections Research Center, accessed April 30, https://exploreuk.uky.edu/fa/findingaid/?id=xt7bg7373d27.

5. Simpson, *Josephine Clay*, 64.

6. "Biography/History."

7. Josephine Clay, "Who Rode La Sylphide?," excerpted in Simpson, *Josephine Clay*, 101–106.

8. Simpson, *Josephine Clay*, 64.

9. "Mrs. Clay's Will," *Richmond Daily Register*, April 6, 1920, 4.

10. Emma Fetta, "Her Success as Horse Breeder," *New York Times*, July 16, 1922, XX2.

11. Fetta, "Her Success as Horse Breeder," XX2.

12. "Only Woman Jockey," *Huntington Herald* (IN), January 21, 1924, 7.

13. "A Female Jockey," *Evening Bee* (Sacramento), October 3, 1891, 2.

14. "Notes of the Turf," n.p., October 4, 1898.

15. "World's Only Woman Jockey," *Daily Herald*, November 1898, 3.

16. "Society Woman as Jockey," *Tennessean*, August 3, 1905, 5.

17. "Indiana Boasts of a Handsome Woman Jockey," *Dayton Herald*, October 22, 1903, 8.

18. "Women and Fast Horses," *Washington Post*, October 7, 1894, 15.

19. "Australian Girl Amazes By Bareback Riding Feats," *The Sun*, April 28, 1912, 13.

20. "Woman in the Stalls," *Chicago Tribune*, July 29, 1896, 10.

21. "Will the Derby of 1910 Be Won by a Woman?," *The Sketch*, May 19, 1909, 171.

22. "The Girl Jockey of the Western States, Dorothy Kincel, Out for a Morning 'Breather,'" *The Sketch*, May 19, 1909, 171.

23. "Girl Jockey Winning Races," *Washington Post*, April 11, 1909, M8.

24. "Horse Carries Woman Rider into River," *Reno Gazette-Journal*, September 2, 1913, 1.

25. "Girl Jockey Grabs Hat," *New York Times*, September 17, 1915, 8; "Woman Jockey in Fair Races," *Daily Advance* (Elizabeth City, NC), November 10, 1919, 1.

26. "Woman Jockey Fell," *The Gazette* (Montreal, CA), November 22, 1919, 22.

27. "Prince George's Girls Thrill the Turf Fans," *Baltimore Sun*, August 20, 1920, 9.

28. "Girl Jockey Made Good Time," *Buffalo Enquirer*, June 30, 1911, 8.

29. "War Conditions," *Cody (NE) Cow Boy*, August 23, 1918, 5.

30. AP, "Calif. Woman Jockey Is Injured by Horse," *Los Angeles Evening Express*, August 29, 1923, 13.

31. "Cowgirl Applies for Jockey License," *Chicago Daily Tribune*, June 20, 1922, 14.

32. "Girl Takes Jockey's Place," *Baltimore Sun*, March 16, 1919, B2.

33. Alden Hatch, "Racing Dynasty," *Country Life*, April 1940, 40; Elizabeth Bent, "She Breeds Great Horses," *New York Times*, December 30, 1923, XX6.

34. Hatch, "Racing Dynasty," 40; Bent, "She Breeds Great Horses," XX6.

35. "Obituary: Miss Elizabeth Daingerfield," *Blood-Horse*, December 15, 1951, 1319; Bent, "She Breeds Great Horses," XX6.

36. Ed Johnstone, "Her Kind Pass Your Way Just Once," *Blood-Horse*, November 22, 1951, 23.

37. "How Castleton Yearlings Learn to Race," *Daily Racing Form*, July 17, 1908, 1.

38. "Castleton Stud," *Daily Racing Form*, November 22, 1901, 1, 5.

39. Elizabeth Daingerfield, "High Stud Fees Menace Turf," *Thoroughbred Record*, January 25, 1930, 105; "How Castleton Yearlings Learn," 1.

40. James O' Donnell Bennett, "Man o' War," *Thoroughbred Record*, March 11, 1923, 133.

41. Bent, "She Breeds Great Horses," XX6.

42. Bent, "She Breeds Great Horses," XX6.

43. "Passing of Two Noted Horsemen," *Colman's Rural World*, January 16, 1913, 66.

44. "Woman Manages Famous Breeding Farm," *San Francisco Call*, January 12, 1913, 11.

45. "A Visit to Kingston Farm," *Thoroughbred Record*, October 21, 1916, 198; "Woman Manages Stud," *Lexington Herald*, April 15, 1917, 12.

46. "Ultimus," accessed February 16, 2023, http://www.americanclassicpedigrees.com/ultimus.html.

47. "Woman Manages Famous Breeding Farm," 11.

48. "Woman Manages Stud," *Lexington Herald*, April 15, 1917, 12.

49. "Passing of Two Noted Horsemen," 66.

50. "New Industry Established at Famous Kingston Farm," *Lexington Herald*, February 16, 1913.

51. "Fifteen Great Mares and Foals Are Burned," *Lexington Herald*, April 30, 1913, 1.

52. "A Visit to Kingston Farm," 198.

53. "May Remain in Charge," *Courier-Journal*, September 4, 1913, 6; "Famous Castleton Stud Is Saved," September 4, 1913, *Lexington Herald*, 1.

54. "Yearling Sale at Lexington," *Daily Racing Form*, March 11, 1914, 1.

55. "Gossip from Blue Grass Region," *Daily Racing Form*, March 21, 1915, 1.

56. "A Visit to Kingston Farm," 198.

57. "Wickliffe Colts Arrive at Gravesend," *Daily Racing Form*, July 14, 1917, 1.

58. "Domino's Staying Progeny," *Thoroughbred Record*, September 17, 1921, 146.

59. "A Visit to Kingston Farm," 198.

60. Sidney Sutherland, "Man o' War and His Dynasty," *Liberty Magazine*, August 28, 1926, 33.

61. "A Word for The Comfort of The Horse," *Lexington Herald*, April 15, 1917, 12.

62. Elizabeth Daingerfield, "Racing's Future Lies in Sportsmen's Hands," *Washington Post*, January 5, 1919, SP1.

63. "Man o' War's Custodian," *The Saratogian*, February 1, 1921, 6.

Notes to Pages 77–82   157

64. "A Woman Now Manages Man o' War," *St. Louis Post-Dispatch*, July 4, 1926, 65.

65. "Superlative Americans," *Chicago Tribune*, March 11, 1923, 132; "Daingerfield Groom Is Tradition's Heir," *Courier-Journal*, May 6, 1939, 48.

66. "Wisdom in Tabloid," *Evening Leader*, February 29, 1924, 4.

67. "Breeders the World Over After the J. E. Widener Nursery Brood-Mares," *Brooklyn Daily Eagle*, March 22, 1925, D5.

68. "Breeders the World Over," D5.

69. "Greatest of Modern Dispersal Sales at Kingston Farm Today," *Lexington Herald*, January 15, 1918, 6.

70. "Ultimus Is Dead," *Brooklyn Daily Eagle*, August 19, 1921, 17.

71. "Miss Daingerfield to Sell Yearlings," *New York Herald*, August 3, 1919, 22.

72. "Man o' War Coddled," *Logansport Pharos-Tribune*, February 28, 1921, 8.

73. "Man o' War Coddled," 8.

74. "Bob Davis Recalls," 8.

75. "How Old Is Auntie?," *Ponca City (OK) News* , April 11, 1921, 3.

76. "'Fans' Mourn Woman Jockey," *Afro-American*, December 20, 1924, 8.

77. "Aunt Eliza Carpenter," *Independence Daily Reporter*, September 10, 1887, 4.

78. "Novelty Race 1 ½ Miles," *Winfield Courier*, July 16, 1891, 6.

79. "Aunt Eliza Carpenter," *Arkansas City (KS) Daily Traveler*, August 5, 1905, 2.

80. "Old Aunt Eliza Carpenter," *Weekly Republican-Traveler* (Arkansas City, KS), April 12, 1894, 5.

81. "Last Night, Aunt Eliza Carpenter," *Arkansas City (KS) Daily Traveler*, June 28, 1897, 5.

82. "Aunt Eliza Carpenter," *Arkansas City (KS) Daily News*, August 1, 1906, 4.

83. "Thousands Enjoyed 101 Ranch Celebration," *Woodward (OK) News*, September 28, 1906, 2.

84. "Thousands Enjoyed," 2.

85. "Big Crowd at Bliss," *Stillwater* (OK) *Gazette* , September 21, 1906, 5; "Thousands Enjoyed," 2.

86. "The Cowboy Passing Away," *Kansas City Star*, September 24, 1906, 3.

87. "'Fans' Mourn," 8.

88. "Man o' War's Yearlings Are Ready for Training," *Owensboro Gazette*, June 28, 1923, 7.

89. Elizabeth Daingerfield, "High Stud Fees Menace Turf," *Thoroughbred Record*, January 25, 1930, 105.

90. "Man o' War Tenant of Fine Quarters," *New York Times*, February 2, 1921, 19.

91. "Miss Daingerfield Predicts," *Courier-Journal*, October 22, 1938, 45.

92. "Morvich a Great Horse, Says Miss Daingerfield," *Washington Post*, December 18, 1922, 13; Peter Burnaugh, "Jockey Club Elects Ryan," *Evening Telegram*, December 15, 1922, 13.

93. "Bob Davis Recalls," 8.

158   Notes to Pages 82–89

94. "Turf Gaining Popularity Despite Business World," *Poughkeepsie Eagle-News*, May 18, 1922, 3.

95. "Small Boys Visit Famous Race Horse," *Lexington Herald*, October 20, 1921, 1–2.

96. Jonathan Brooks, "Famous Racer Carrier $500,000 of Insurance," *Brooklyn Daily Eagle*, June 20, 1930, 4.

97. "Steadfast Wins Name Handicap," *New York Telegram*, March 2, 1924, 19.

98. "Miss Elizabeth Daingerfield," *Thoroughbred Record*, December 28, 1940, 442.

99. Dorothy Ours, *Man o' War* (New York: St. Martin's, 2006), 216; "Turf Hallmarks," accessed February 16, 2023, http://www.tbheritage.com/TurfHallmarks/racecharts/USA/Futurity.html.

100. "Gives Up Man o' War," *New York Sun*, October 11, 1930, n.p.

101. "Miss Daingerfield 'On the Air,'" *Thoroughbred Record*, April 2, 1932.

102. "A Lady's Views," *Blood-Horse*, June 18, 1832, 825.

103. Rena Niles, "When We Went Out to the West Coast," *Courier-Journal*, January 1, 1939, 38.

104. "Obituary," 1319.

105. "Honor Dixie Horsewoman," *Los Angeles Times*, June 2, 1923, III2.

106. Robert Dundon, "Women in Care of Great Horses," *Lexington Leader*, April 17, 1921, 6.

107. "Lucky Hour's Dam Is Dead," *Blood-Horse*, April 14, 1922, 1; "Numerous Thoroughbred Foals Reported During the Past Week in Bluegrass," *Lexington Herald*, March 10, 1918, 8; "About Women," *Mound City Journal*, February 12, 1925, 4.

108. "Great Interest Manifested Here in Nursery Stud Dispersal to Be Held May 15," *Lexington Herald*, March 22, 1925, 5.

109. "A. A. Pons Leases the Nursery Farm," *Lexington Leader*, May 21, 1925, 5.

110. "Lucky Hour's Dam Is Dead," 1; "Numerous Thoroughbred Foals," 8.

111. "Bob Davis Recalls," 8.

5. Cowgirls

1. "An Oregon Amazon," *Atlanta Constitution*, June 16, 1888, 4.

2. "Mysterious Horsewoman of New Mexico," *Chicago Daily Tribune*, October 21, 1906, D1.

3. Winifred Gallagher, *The New Woman in the Old West* (New York: Penguin, 2021), 78.

4. "Female Cowboy in the Sioux Lands," *Chicago Daily Tribune*, June 15, 1893, 11.

5. Gallagher, *The New Woman in the Old West*, 94.

6. Rebecca Scofield, *Outriders: Rodeo at the Fringes of the American West* (Seattle: Washington UP, 2019), 28.

7. Michael Allen, "The Rise and Decline of the Early Rodeo Cowgirl," *Pacific Northwest Quarterly* 83, no. 4 (October 1992): 123.

Notes to Pages 89–97   159

8. Renee Laegreid, "Rodeo Queens at the Pendleton Round-Up," *Oregon Historical Quarterly* 104, no. 1 (Spring 2003): 6–23.

9. Glenda Riley, "Annie Oakley: Creating the Cowgirl," *Montana: The Magazine of Western History* 45, no. 3 (Summer 1995): 32–47.

10. "Female Cowboy," 11.

11. "Female Cowboy," 11.

12. "Bronco Kate," *Los Angeles Times*, July 28, 1892, 2.

13. "Daring Woman Horse Thief," *Chicago Daily Tribune*, May 3, 1896, 37.

14. "Are Great Hunters," *New York World*, May 31, 1902, n.p.

15. "They Both Knew Her," *The Times* (Philadelphia), August 11, 1889, 14; "Cattle Kate's Career," *National Police Gazette*, August 10, 1889, 6.

16. "They Both Knew Her," 14.

17. "Miscellaneous," *Great Bend Weekly Tribune*, September 20, 1889, 1.

18. "Lynched by Cowboys," *Evening Bulletin* (Maysville, KY), July 23, 1889, 1.

19. "Woman and a Horse Thief," *San Bernadino*, n.d., n.p.

20. "Woman and a Horse Thief," n.p.

21. "Cora the Cowgirl," *Chicago Daily Tribune*, March 2, 1902, 54.

22. "Cora the Cowgirl," 54.

23. Allen, "The Rise and Decline," 123; Liz Stiffler and Tom Blake, "Fannie Sperry-Steele: Montana's Champion Bronc Rider," *Montana: The Magazine of Western History* 32, no. 2 (Spring 1982): 44–57.

24. Stiffler and Blake, "Fannie Sperry-Steele," 48.

25. Stiffler and Blake, "Fannie Sperry-Steele," 56.

26. "Fatal Accident to Woman Rider in Wild West Show," *Topeka State Journal*, May 14, 1901, 4.

27. "A Kansas Cowgirl's Fate," *New York Times*, December 27, 1897, 6.

28. "Zach Mulhall of Oklahoma," *Wichita Beacon*, November 21, 1900, 3.

29. "Miss Mulhall at the Reunion," *Wichita Daily Eagle*, July 11, 1900, 2.

30. "A Girl's Fearless Riding," *Times-Democrat*, October 15, 1899, 10.

31. Rose Marion, "The Athletic Girl of the Plains," *St. Louis Post-Dispatch*, October 19, 1902, 1.

32. "Miss Mulhall at El Paso," *Arizona Republic*, March 14, 1903, 10.

33. "How Bossie Mulhall Became Queen of the Range," *San Francisco Chronicle*, November 1, 1903, 5.

34. "Miss Mulhall, Belle of Oklahoma, Lariat Expert," *New York Times*, April 9, 1905, SM5; "'Bossie' Mulhall Holds World Record for Steer Roping," *St. Louis Republic*, October 12, 1902, 16.

35. "Carnival at Fair Grounds," *St. Louis Post-Dispatch*, October 9, 1899, 7.

36. "A Girl's Fearless Riding," 10.

37. "Miss Mulhall at the Reunion," *Wichita Daily Eagle*, July 11, 1900, 2.

38. Marion, "The Athletic Girl of the Plains," 1.

39. "'Bossie' Mulhall Holds World Record," 16.

40. "Cowpuncher Queen," *Wichita Daily Eagle*, April 30, 1905, 22.

160   Notes to Pages 97–100

41. "Lucille Mulhall, 'Queen of the Cowboys,' Hurt in Riding Contest," *The Evening World*, October 13, 1902, 4.

42. "Lucille Mulhall," *Wichita Daily Beacon*, February 13, 1902, 6.

43. "'Bossie' Mulhall Holds World Record for Steer Roping," *St. Louis Republic*, October 12, 1902, 16.

44. "Virgie D'Or," accessed February 18, 2023, https://www.pedigreequery.com/virgie+dor.

45. "Fair Cattle Queen Fights for Her Pet," *Indianapolis News*, November 2, 1903, 7.

46. "Was a Fitting Climax," *Wichita Daily Beacon*, February 14, 1902, 5.

47. "Woman Rider Is Injured in Race at Fair Grounds," *St. Louis Republic*, October 13, 1902, 1.

48. "Woman Rider Is Injured," 1.

49. "Miss Lucille Mulhall Falls from Pony," *Chanute Daily Tribune*, October 13, 1902, 1.

50. Rose Marion, "Miss Mulhall Badly Injured," *St. Louis Post-Dispatch*, October 13, 1902, 1.

51. "Miss Mulhall Recovers," *St. Louis Post-Dispatch*, October 17, 1902, 3; "Cowboys Take Possession of a Theater," *St. Louis Post-Dispatch*, November 2, 1902, 1.

52. "Miss Mulhall, Belle of Oklahoma, Lariat Expert," *New York Times*, April 9, 1905, SM5.

53. "Cowboys Coaching Go," *New York Tribune*, May 2, 1905, 8.

54. Mary Edith Day, "A Ranch Girl," *The Sun* (Chanute, KS), January 16, 1904, 2.

55. "Cowgirls Ride Up Avenue," *New York Times*, April 24, 1905, 9; "Colonel Zach Mulhall and the Western Cowboys," *Wilkes-Barre Times*, April 27, 1905, 7.

56. "Cowgirls Ride Up Avenue," 9.

57. "Convent Girl the Star of the Wild West Show," *Chicago Daily Tribune*, May 15, 1910, B6.

58. Marion, "The Athletic Girl of the Plains," 1.

59. "Thrilling Entertainment is Promised at Fair Grounds Today," *St. Louis Post-Dispatch*, May 3, 1903, 15; Charles Furlong, *Let 'Er Buck* (New York: Putnam, 1921), 169.

60. Congress of Rough Riders of the World, advertisement, *Kinsley Mercury* (Kinsley, KS), January 30, 1903, 6.

61. "President's Cowboy Friend," *Charlotte News*, October 8, 1903, 1.

62. "Woman Won," *Decatur Herald*, October 9, 1903, 1.

63. "Three Pikers Shot," *Galveston Daily News*, June 19, 1904, 3.

64. "Zach Mulhall Shoots Three in Crowd on Pike," *St. Louis Post-Dispatch*, June 19, 1904, 1.

65. "Mulhall Out, Butler Signs a $20,000 Bond," *St. Louis Post-Dispatch*, June 20, 1904, 1.

66. "Cattle King Gives Bonds," *San Francisco Call*, June 21, 1904, 5.

67. "Mulhall Convicted of Shooting," *St. Louis Post-Dispatch* January 26, 1905, 9.

68. "Police Benefit," advertisement, *St. Louis Post-Dispatch*, November 12, 1904, 10.

Notes to Pages 100–105   161

69. "Disgrace to Oklahoma," *Guthrie Daily Leader*, April 24, 1905, 1.

70. "Disgrace to Oklahoma," 1.

71. "At the Horse Fair," *Brooklyn Daily Eagle*, April 27, 1905, 11.

72. "Lucille Mulhall and Her Trained Horse, 'Governor,'" *Coffeyville Daily Journal*, August 19, 1905, 1.

73. "Wild Steer Cause of Theater Panic," *St. Louis Post-Dispatch*, April 28, 1905, 11.

74. "Cowboy Loses His Suit against Miss Mulhall," *St. Louis Post-Dispatch*, May 19, 1908, 1.

75. "Kept Marriage a Secret," *Scranton Republican*, October 22, 1908, 1.

76. "Lucille Mulhall, Queen of Bronco Busters," *The Inter Ocean*, May 15, 1910, 36.

77. "Hardware Men Saw Wild West Houston," *Houston Post*, April 19, 1917, 7.

78. "Queen of Rodeo Gives Up Spurs," *Greenfield Daily Reporter*, June 30, 1922, 3.

79. "Now Booking Fair Season for 1916," advertisement, *Billboard*, April 29, 1916, 65.

80. "So This Is Mulhall!" *Wichita Beacon*, November 5, 1922, 8C.

81. "Zach Mulhall, a Pioneer of the Southwest, Dead," *Sedalia Democrat*, September 18, 1931, 1.

82. "Queen of the Plains," *Pampa (TX) Sunday News-Post*, November 11, 1931, 3.

83. "Tames the Wildest Horses," *Baltimore Sun*, November 3, 1901, 11.

84. "Tames the Wildest Horses," 11.

85. "Experience as a Trainer of Mustangs," *New York Times*, June 10, 1906, X4.

86. "Experience as a Trainer of Mustangs," X4.

87. "Equestrienne Gives a Park Matinee," *New York Times*, May 2, 1910, 9.

88. "Story of Sioux Princess Wenona with 101 Ranch Wild West Show," *The Independent*, November 16, 1911, 6.

89. "Friends Rally to Bier of One Who Was 'Crack' Shot," *The Courier* (Waterloo, IA), February 4, 1930, 18.

90. "Princess Wenona, Girl with Wild West Show, Has Had Adventures," *Lansing State Journal*, July 12, 1913, 9.

91. "Pittsburg's First Hippodrome," *Woman's Magazine of the Greater Sunday Press* (Pittsburgh), July 25, 1909, 5.

92. "Romance of a Princess," *Evening Star* (Independence, KS), September 22, 1913, 3.

93. "Princess Wenona," *Corsicana Daily Sun* (Corsicana, TX), October 13, 1913, 7.

94. "Princess Wenona Died," *Miami Herald*, February 11, 1930, 6.

95. Stiffler and Blake, "Fannie Sperry-Steele," 50.

96. Stiffler and Blake, "Fannie Sperry-Steele," 50.

97. Stiffler and Blake, "Fannie Sperry-Steele," 47.

98. "The Champion Rough Rider Who Never Saw a Ranch," *The Times* (Shreveport, LA), September 10, 1916, 29.

99. Stiffler and Blake, "Fannie Sperry-Steele," 56.

100. "Romantic Notions of Cowgirls Gone," *Chicago Defender*, September 30, 1911, 8.

162   Notes to Pages 105–112

101. "Kitty Canutt of Round-Up Loses Gem from Tooth," *Oregon Daily Journal*, October 31, 1920, 11.

102. Furlong, *Let 'Er Buck*, 29.

103. Furlong, *Let 'Er Buck*, 187.

104. Furlong, *Let 'Er Buck*, 195.

105. Furlong, *Let 'Er Buck*, 75.

106. Allen, "The Rise and Decline," 124.

107. Allen, "The Rise and Decline," 127.

108. Allen, "The Rise and Decline," 126.

109. "Girl Scares Cowboys but Subdues 'Bucker,'" *Los Angeles Times*, March 5, 1912, III2.

110. "Pepless Gothamites Bore This Cowgirl," *Los Angeles Times*, December 6, 1920, I4.

111. "She Would Be Cowgirl," *Baltimore Sun*, July 21, 1909, 12.

112. Furlong, *Let 'Er Buck*, 7.

113. "Bachelor Cow-girls," *Washington Post*, November 23, 1902, 32.

6. Circus Riders

1. Joseph Bottum and Justin L. Blessinger, "The American Circus in All Its Glory," *Humanities*, Fall 2018, https://www.neh.gov/article/american-circus-all-its-glory.

2. Isaac Greenwood, *The Circus: Its Origin and Growth Prior to 1835* (New York: Dunlap Society, 1909), 19.

3. Greenwood, *The Circus*, 33.

4. Les Standiford, *Battle for the Big Top* (New York: Hachette, 2021), 15; Greenwood, *The Circus*, 52.

5. Susanna Forrest, "The 'Princess Daredevil' of the Belle Epoque," accessed February 20, 2023, https://www.theparisreview.org/blog/columns/ecuyeres/.

6. "Alas for the Circus Lady," *The Sun*, April 12, 1896, 28.

7. Janet M. Davis, *The Circus Age* (Chapel Hill: North Carolina UP, 2002), 240.

8. Davis, *The Circus Age*, 141.

9. Davis, *The Circus Age*, 21.

10. "Ringling Bros and Barnum & Bailey Combined Shoes," poster, 1910, https://www.icanvas.com/canvas-print/1910-ringling-bros-and-barnum-bailey-circus-poster-taa.

11. "Miss May Wirth," poster, accessed April 25, 2024, https://hdl.huntington.org/digital/collection/p16003coll4/id/2034.

12. Davis, *The Circus Age*, 80.

13. "Over 700 Horses in Biggest Circus," *Washington Post*, May 8, 1919, 11.

14. "A Day in the Life of a Circus Horse," *Chicago Tribune*, September 19, 1901, 63.

15. "Favorite Mount Drew Hearse," *Buffalo Evening News*, June 10, 1927, 34.

16. "Nearly Starved in Alaska," *Baltimore Sun*, May 18, 1906, 14.

17. Walter Anthony, "Miss May Wirth," *San Francisco Call*, September 8, 1912, 25.

18. "Circus Women," *Los Angeles Times*, July 25, 1897, 20.

Notes to Pages 112–116   163

19. "Circus Women," 20.

20. Margaret Mayo, *Polly of the Circus* (New York: A. L. Burt, 1908), 9.

21. Mayo, *Polly of the Circus*, 17.

22. Mayo, *Polly of the Circus*, 69.

23. Mayo, *Polly of the Circus*, 111.

24. "Young Boys Burglars?," *Baltimore Sun*, December 31, 1903, 9.

25. "The Youngest Girl Circus Rider," *Chicago Daily Tribune*, April 13, 1913, B6.

26. "Training Circus Horses," *Woodland (CA) Daily Democrat*, June 27, 1891, 1.

27. "The Training of Athletes," *Pittsburgh Daily Post*, September 19, 1897, 7.

28. Cleveland Moffett, "The Fascinating Art of the Circus Rider," *Atlanta Constitution*, June 9, 1895, 32.

29. "May Wirth," *Billboard*, February 12, 1921, 66; "May Wirth Headlines Bill Opening at Proctor's Today," *Yonkers Statesman and News*, January 18, 1923.

30. "Mother Abandons May Wirth," *New York Sun*, April 2, 1926, 29.

31. "May Wirth," accessed April 16, 2022, http://www.circopedia.org/May_Wirth; "May Wirth, Horse-Act," *Variety*, November 19, 1914, 17.

32. "Famous Rider Carries Big Stable on Tour," *Atlanta Constitution*, September 15, 1918, 12.

33. "Favorite Mount Drew Hearse," 34.

34. "Circus Folks," *Buffalo Evening News*, June 11, 1927, 7.

35. "Bareback Rider Fears Cab Horses," *Philadelphia Inquirer*, May 4, 1919, n.p.

36. "Invisible Watch Her Secret Says Fair Rider," *South Bend News-Tribune*, July 28, 1920, 9.

37. "Circus Rider Asked to Write a History," *New York Times*, April 4, 1920, E10.

38. "Australian Girl Amazes by Bareback Riding Feats," 1912, *New York Sun*, April 28, 1912, 53.

39. "Bareback Rider Fears Cab Horses," n.p.

40. "Bareback Rider Fears Cab Horses," n.p.

41. "Australian Girl Amazes by Bareback Riding Feats," *The Sun* (New York), April 28, 1912, 53.

42. "Australian Girl Amazes by Bareback Riding Feats," 53.

43. "Australian Girl Amazes by Bareback Riding Feats," 53.

44. "Australian Girl Amazes by Bareback Riding Feats," 53.

45. "Circus Horse Imparts News," *Evening Telegram*, April 9, 1920, 10.

46. "Circus Rider Asked to Write a History," E10.

47. "Australian Girl Amazes by Bareback Riding Feats," 1912, Fulton History file, need to find.

48. "Barnum and Bailey Show Opens," *Billboard*, March 30, 1912, 1; Anthony, "Miss May Wirth," 25.

49. "May Wirth Badly Hurt," *New York Times*, April 23, 1913, 1.

50. "Horse Nearly Kills Circus Rider," April 24, 1913, 3.

51. "May Wirth, Circus Rider, Recovering," *Brooklyn Daily Eagle*, April 23, 1913, 3.

164 Notes to Pages 116–119

52. "Horse Nearly Kills Circus Rider," 3.

53. "May Wirth Badly Hurt," 1.

54. "May Wirth," *Billboard*, November 29, 1913, 21.

55. "May Wirth," 21.

56. "Supercircus Draws Crowds to Garden," *New York Times*, March 30, 1919, 25.

57. "Bareback Rider Fears Cab Horses," n.p.

58. "Palace Bill Is Thrilling," *Billboard*, February 28, 1920, 369.

59. Standiford, *Battle for the Big Top*, 185; "Circus Rider Asked to Write a History," E10.

60. "Invisible Watch Her Secret Says Fair Rider," 9.

61. "May Wirth Rides a Bull," *New York Times*, November 10, 1922, 18.

62. "Babe Ruth Astride King Jess," photograph, Getty Images, accessed February 20, 2023, https://www.gettyimages.com/detail/news-photo/american-baseball -player-babe-ruth-waves-his-cap-while-news-photo/84196436.

63. "Mary [*sic*] Wirth Doing Handstand on a Bull," photograph, Getty Images, accessed February 20, 2023, https://www.gettyimages.com/detail/news-photo /harrington-park-nj-mary-wirth-the-famous-bare-back-rider-of-news-photo /530835112.

64. Thomas L. Stokes, "Coolidge Puts Cares Aside," *Atlanta Constitution*, May 14, 1924, 7.

65. "Role in Musical Comedy Great Hope of May Wirth," *Binghamton Press*, May 26, 1931, 3.

66. "Circus Shrine Honors Famed Equestrienne," *Indianapolis Star*, September 13, 1964, 108.

67. "A Pleasing Equestrian Act," *Pittsburgh Daily Post*, September 29, 1907, 35; "Stage and Canvas," *Boston Globe*, June 12, 1894, 2.

68. "Fascinating Equestriennes in Friendly Rivalry," *Chattanooga News*, June 9, 1906, 4.

69. "A Pleasing Equestrian Act," 35; "Fascinating Equestriennes in Friendly Rivalry," 4.

70. "Pretty Rose Wentworth," *New York Times*, April 28, 1895, 16.

71. "Rose Wentworth Equestrian Sensation," *Washington Times*, February 2, 1905, 4; "Vaudeville at Poli's," *Hartford Courant*, April 4, 1906, 7.

72. "Mary Norman and Other Vaudeville Features at Chase's," *Washington Post*, February 5, 1905, 7.

73. "There Is Variety in Plenty," *Philadelphia Inquirer*, January 7, 1906, 36; "At the Shows," *Boston Globe*, January 18, 1906, 12.

74. "Circus Queen Quits," *Detroit Free Press*, December 15, 1905, 12.

75. "Ex-Circus Star Recalls," *The Landmark*, October 7, 1937, 6.

76. "Rose Wentworth Carr and Major Bob Yokum's Great Buffalo Exhibition," *Vancouver Sun*, September 23, 1912, 18.

77. "Patterson Carnival Proves Aggregation of Clean Attractions," *Weekly Times-Record*, August 7, 1913, 1.

Notes to Pages 119–123   165

78. "Bisons Can't Land," *Evening Sun*, April 3, 1914, 8.

79. "A Life among Horses Has a Charm for Mme. Marantette," *New York Times*, April 12, 1903, 28; "How Horses Are Taught Tricks," *Chicago Daily Tribune*, June 22, 1897, 10.

80. "Circus Rider's Will Directs That She Be Buried with Her Dog," *Washington Post*, January 29, 1922, 1; "A Life among Horses Has a Charm for Mme. Marantette," 28.

81. "Miss Peek," *Los Angeles Times*, December 29, 1888, 2.

82. "A Life among Horses Has a Charm for Mme. Marantette," 28.

83. "Circus Rider's Will Directs That She Be Buried with Her Dog," 1; "A Life among Horses Has a Charm for Mme. Marantette," 28; Anna Sochocky, "Setting a Side-Saddle Jumping Record," *Untacked Magazine*, Winter 2021, 62.

84. "How Horses Are Taught Tricks," 10.

85. "Wonderful Horsewoman," *The Billboard*, March 23, 1813, 141.

86. "Circus Rider's Will Directs That She Be Buried with Her Dog," 1; "A Life among Horses Has a Charm for Mme. Marantette," 28.

87. "How Horses Are Taught Tricks," 10.

88. "How Horses Are Taught Tricks," 10; "Horse Jumping Feats," *Baltimore Sun*, December 30, 1903, 9.

89. "How to Ride Jumpers," *Baltimore Sun*, November 24, 1903, 9.

90. "How Horses Are Taught Tricks," 10.

91. "How Horses Are Taught Tricks," 10.

92. "A Life among Horses Has a Charm for Mme. Marantette," 28.

93. "How to Ride Jumpers," 9.

94. "How to Ride Jumpers," 9.

95. Standiford, *Battle for the Big Top*, 181.

96. Tody Hamilton, "Wages of Circus People Are Far from Princely," *Baltimore Sun*, January 12, 1908, 13; "How to Ride Jumpers," 9.

97. "Wonderful Horsewoman," 141.

98. "Wonderful Horsewoman," 141.

99. "Wonderful Horsewoman," 141.

100. "Circus Rider's Will Directs That She Be Buried with Her Dog," 1.

101. "Suffragists at Tea with Circus Women," *New York Times*, April 8, 1912, 7.

102. "Suffragists at Tea," 7.

103. "Enlist Suffragists for a Circus Holiday," *New York Times*, April 1, 1912, 7.

104. "Enlist Suffragists," 7.

105. "New Feats Startle," *New York Times*, March 20, 1908, 7.

106. "Burlesque 'Balloon Horse'" *Variety*, October 2, 1909, 15.

107. "Mrs. C.M. Robinson, Once Circus Star," *New York Times*, March 10, 1948, 27.

108. "A Child of the Circus," *Christian Science Monitor*, August 25, 1926, 8.

109. "Mrs. C.M. Robinson," 27; Fox 60.

110. "Star of the Past Haunts the Circus," *New York Times*, April 16, 1935, 26.

111. "Mrs. C.M. Robinson," 27.

166 Notes to Pages 123–129

112. Josie Demott, "The Real Woman of the Circus," *Washington Post*, May 13, 1906, EA6.

113. "Nearly Starved in Alaska," 14.

114. "Mrs. C.M. Robinson," 27.

115. "Star of the Past," 26.

116. "Youth Possible to Every Woman Who Really Wants It," *New York Times*, February 16, 1913, 44.

117. "Mrs. C.M. Robinson," 27.

118. "Star of the Past," 26.

7. Extreme Riding

1. Florence Shinkle, "Across Nation by Horse is a Long Ride," *St. Louis Post-Dispatch*, August 22, 2005, JC1.

2. Elizabeth Letts, *The Ride of Her Life* (New York: Ballantine, 2021).

3. "Woman Mail Carrier," *Washington Post*, July 23, 1899, 26.

4. "A Virginia New Woman," *Washington Post*, March 12, 1898, 3.

5. "Dashing Girls," *Los Angeles Times*, June 9, 1883, 6.

6. "Horseback Girls in the Yosemite," *Los Angeles Times*, August 3, 1916, III1.

7. "Three Rival Horsewomen," *Washington Post*, August 25, 1881, 3.

8. "Three Rival Horsewomen," 3.

9. "Three Rival Horsewomen," 3.

10. Mary Higginbotham, *In Genuine Cowgirl Style* (n.p.: Long Riders' Guild, 2007), 27.

11. "'Montana Girl' Champion Lariat Twirler," *Anaconda Standard* (Anaconda, MT), June 28, 1925, 34; "Nan Aspinwall Back from Her Record-Breaking Ride," *Butte Miner*, April 29, 1912, 8.

12. "From Ocean to Ocean on Horseback," *Muskogee Times-Democrat*, September 21, 1910, 5.

13. "Cowgirl Shoots Up Town," *Washington Post*, December 23, 1910, 1.

14. "Nan Aspinwall on Her Way," *Evening Bulletin* (Honolulu), March 15, 1911, 10.

15. Higginbotham, *In Genuine Cowgirl Style*, 51.

16. "Nan Aspinwall on Her Way," 10.

17. "Mare Saves Life of Cowgirl," *St. Louis Post-Dispatch*, April 14, 1911, 15.

18. "Nan Aspinwall on Her Way," 10.

19. "Girl Rides Across Continent," *Washington Post*, July 6, 1911, 7.

20. "Girl Ends Long Horseback Ride," *Los Angeles Times*, July 9, 1911, 19.

21. "Girl Ends Long Ride," *Boston Globe*, July 9, 1911, 4.

22. "Girl Ends Long Horseback Ride," 19.

23. "Can't Get Excited," *Leavenworth (KS) Times*, July 18, 1911, 4.

24. "Nan J. Aspinwall, 'The Montana Girl,' in Town," *Morning Call* (Allentown, PA), September 18, 1911, 8.

25. "Nan Aspinwall Back from Her Record-Breaking Ride," 8.

26. "Has a Horse That Crossed the Continent," *Courier News-Register* (Bridgewater, NJ), August 3, 1914, 2.

27. "Lost Reynaed at Daven Woods," *Buffalo Sunday Morning News*, October 26, 1902, 9.

28. "American Women in Politics," *Times and Democrat* (South Carolina), April 25, 1907, 7; "Club History," Sulgrave Club, accessed February 20, 2023, https://www.sulgraveclub.org/the-club/club-history.

29. Lida Fleitmann Bloodgood, *Hoofs in the Distance* (New York: Van Nostrand, 1953), 95.

30. "Are Nearing Home," *Buffalo Morning Express*, June 2, 1907, 14.

31. "Party Begins Long Ride," *Washington Post*, May 11, 1909, 7.

32. Judith H. Lanius and Sharon C. Park, "Martha Wadsworth's Mansion," *Washington History* 7, no. 1 (Spring/Summer 1995): 24; "Long Trip on Horseback," *New York Tribune*, May 11, 1909, 6.

33. "Mrs. Herbert Wadsworth is Making Her Annual 1,000 Mile Horseback Ride," *Post-Crescent* (Wisconsin), May 6, 1912, 1.

34. "She Ends 900-Mile Ride," *Washington Post*, May 28, 1912, 1.

35. "Mrs. Herbert Wadsworth, Society Leader," *Rutland Daily Herald*, June 22, 1909, 1; Lanius and Park, "Martha Wadsworth's Mansion," 27; "She Outdoes T. Roosevelt," *Evening Herald* (Kansas), July 27, 1910, 4.

36. "The World's Record Ride," *Kansas City Times*, July 23, 1910, 4.

37. "Woman's Record Ride," *Washington Evening Star*, July 22, 1910, 2.

38. "Famous Equestriennes," *Washington Post*, September 10, 1910, 2.

39. "Famous Equestriennes," 2.

40. "To Ride with Officers," *Washington Post*, March 6, 1910, E1.

41. "Trousers for Women," *Washington Post*, March 27, 1910, E1.

42. "California Horsewoman on Way to the Atlantic," *Daily Arkansas Gazette*, September 24, 1911, 3.

43. "Girl's 8,100 Mile Ride," *New York Times*, June 29, 1912, 4.

44. Tom Kuipers, "Alberta Claire: The Girl from Wyoming," Urbana Free Library blog, accessed July 19, 2022, https://urbanafreelibrary.org/blogs/2022/03/16/alberta-claire-girl-wyoming.

45. Alberta Claire, "An Incident," *The Teepee*, October 1915, accessed on February 20, 2023, http://www.thelongridersguild.com/alberta.htm.

46. "Facts and Fancies in Woman's World," *Washington Post*, July 3, 1912, 7.

47. "Women on Horseback," *Atlanta Constitution*, July 15, 1882, 1.

48. "Women on Horseback," 1.

49. "Accident to a Girl Rider," *Atlanta Constitution*, August 5, 1883, 7.

50. "A Life among Horses Has a Charm for Mme. Marantette," *New York Times*, April 12, 1903, 28.

51. "Great Preparations," *Algona (IA) Republican*, July 19, 1899, 5.

52. "G.F. Holloway," *Algona (IA) Courier*, September 9, 1898.

53. "Geo. Holloway's Ponies," *Algona (IA) Upper Des Moines*, October 11, 1899, 1.

168 Notes to Pages 136–140

54. "Diving Horses at Island Park," *Fall River Herald*, August 21, 1909, 3.

55. "Geo. Holloway's Ponies," 1.

56. "The Diving Horses," *Evening Star*, September 5, 1900, 10.

57. "King and Queen," advertisement, *Evening Times* (Washington, DC), September 7, 1900, 5.

58. "Fifty Years Ago," *Cincinnati Enquirer*, July 10, 1951, 8.

59. John Corr, "Really Not So Amazing," *Chicago Tribune*, August 25, 1991, 12.

60. "Diving Horse Combination," *St. Joseph Observer*, September 22, 1906, 2; "Dr. Carver's World's Wonder," advertisement, Albuquerque Citizen, July 3, 1906, 6.

61. "Diving Horse Combination," 2.

62. "Dr. Carver's Great Show," *Houston Post*, March 20, 1907, 15.

63. "The Frontier and Harvest Festival Association," *Grand Island (NE) Daily Independent*, September 26, 1908, 3.

64. "Young Lady a Bronco Buster," *Albuquerque Citizen*, June 26, 1906, 5.

65. Sonora Carver, *A Girl and Five Brave Horses* (Mansfield Centre, CT: Martino, 2011), 30.

66. "Girl Dives Forty Feet on Horseback," *Atlanta Constitution*, February 11, 1906, C1.

67. "Dreamland," *Brooklyn Daily Eagle*, June 28, 1908, 18.

68. Kevin Riordan, "Ex-Steel Pier Worker Recalls Era of the Diving Horse," *Courier-Post*, August 4, 1985, 7B.

69. Carver, *A Girl and Five Brave Horses*, 11.

70. Corr, "Really Not So Amazing," 12.

71. Carver, *A Girl and Five Brave Horses*, 14.

72. Jacqueline L. Urgo, "Atlantic City Act: Relic of the Past," *Republican and Herald* (Pottsville, PA), March 4, 2012, C3.

73. "Pittsburg's First Hippodrome," *Woman's Magazine of the Greater Sunday Press* (Pittsburgh), July 25, 1909, 5.

74. "Pittsburg's First Hippodrome," 5.

75. "Diving Horse Act Protested," *Chattanooga News*, October 3, 1922, 7.

Selected Bibliography

Abernathy, Miles. *Ride the Wind: The Amazing True Story of the Abernathy Boys*. n.p.: Long Riders' Guild, 2004.

Alderson, Nannie T. *A Bride Goes West*. Lincoln: Nebraska UP, 1942.

American Club Woman Magazine. New York: American Club Woman Publishing Company, 1916.

Angell, George Thorndike. *Our Dumb Animals*. Boston: Massachusetts Society for the Prevention of Cruelty to Animals, 1919.

Barrett, Major J. L. M. *Practical Jumping*. New York: Scribner's, 1930.

Beach, Belle. *Riding and Driving for Women*. New York: Scribner's, 1912.

Beers, Diane L. *For the Prevention of Cruelty*. Athens: Ohio UP, 2006.

Bit & Spur 4, part 1, January 1907.

Bloodgood, Lida Fleitmann. *Hoofs in the Distance*. New York: Van Nostrand, 1953.

———. *The Saddle of Queens*. London: J. A. Allen, 1959.

Branigan, Cynthia A. *The Last Diving Horse in America*. New York: Pantheon, 2021.

Brown, Dee. *The Gentle Tamers: Women of the Old Wild West*. Lincoln: Nebraska UP, 1958.

Bush, Francis Marion. *Famous Horsewomen of Virginia*. Midlothian, TX: Bush, 2007.

Carlson, Laurie Winn. *On Sidesaddles to Heaven*. Caldwell, ID: Caxton, 1998.

Carter, Allan, and Mike Kane. *150 Years of Racing in Saratoga*. Charleston, SC: History Press, 2013.

Carver, Sonora, as told to Elizabeth Land. *A Girl and Five Brave Horses*. Mansfield Center, CT: Martino, 2011.

Clayton, John. *The Cowboy Girl*. Lincoln: Nebraska UP, 2007.

Daingerfield, Keene. *Training for Fun*. Lexington, KY: Thoroughbred Press, 1948.

Day, Beth. *America's First Cowgirl*. New York: Messner, 1955.

Dunlap, Patricia Riley. *Riding Astride: The Frontier in Women's History*. Denver: Arden, 1995.

170 Selected Bibliography

Durrell, L. W. *A Manual for Riders*. New York: Zeff-Davis, 1949.

Eichler, Victor. *Madame Marantette: Queen of the Saddle*. Three Rivers, MI: Shantamira Press, 2014.

Enss, Chris. *Buffalo Gals: Women of Buffalo Bill's Wild West Show*. Helena, MT: TwoDot, 2006.

―――. *The Doctor Wore Petticoats: Women Physicians of the Old West*. Helena, MT: TwoDot, 2006.

Fishback, Mary. *Northern Virginia's Equestrian Heritage*. Charleston, SC: Arcadia, 2002.

Forrest, Susanna. *If Wishes Were Horses*. London: Atlantic, 2012.

Fox, Charles Philip. *A Pictorial History of Performing Horses*. Seattle: Superior, 1960.

Furlong, Charles Wellington. *Let 'Er Buck*. New York: Putnam, 1921.

Furman, Necah Stewart. *Caroline Lockhart: Her Life and Legacy*. Seattle: Washington UP, 1994.

Gallagher, Winifred. *New Women in the Old West*. New York: Penguin, 2021.

Greene, Ann Norton. *Horses at Work: Harnessing Power in Industrial America*. Cambridge: Harvard UP, 2008.

Gunning, Brooke, and Paige Horine. *Maryland Thoroughbred Racing*. Charleston, SC: Arcadia, 2005.

Halley, Jean O'Malley. *Horse Crazy: Girls and the Lives of Horses*. Athens: Georgia UP, 2019.

Haney, Lynn. *The Lady Is a Jock*. New York: Dodd Mead, 1973.

Hayes, Alice M. *The Horsewoman: A Practical Guide to Side-Saddle Riding*. New York: Scribner's, 1903.

Higginbotham, Mary. *In Genuine Cowgirl Fashion*. n.p.: Long Riders' Guild, 2007.

Katz, William Loren. *Black Women of the Old West*. New York: Atheneum, 1995.

Kelley, Robert F., ed. *The Year Book of the Horse, 1934*. New York: Dodd, Mead, 1935.

Klasner, Lily. *My Girlhood among Outlaws*. 1968. Tucson: Arizona UP, 1988.

LaCompte, Mary Lou. *Cowgirls of the Rodeo*. Urbana: Illinois UP, 1983.

Lepore, Jill. *The Secret History of Wonder Woman*. New York: Vintage, 2015.

Letts, Elizabeth. *The Ride of Her Life*. New York: Ballantine, 2021.

Lowe, Mifflin. *The True West*. Bushel & Peck, 2020.

Luchetti, Cathy. *Women of the West*. St. George, UT: Antelope Island, 1982.

Lumsden, Linda J. *Inez: The Life and Times of Inez Milholland*. Bloomington: Indiana UP, 2004.

Maddison, Ivy. *Riding Astride for Girls*. New York: Henry Holt.

Marcus, Halimah, ed. *Horse Girls*. New York: Harper, 2021.

Marvine, Dee. *The Lady Rode Bucking Horses*. Billings, MT: TwoDot, 2015.

Mayor, Adrienne. *The Amazons*. Princeton, NJ: Princeton UP, 2014.

McEvoy, John, and Julia McEvoy. *Women in Racing in Their Own Words*. Lexington, KY: Eclipse, 2001.

Selected Bibliography   171

McShane, Clay, and Joel A. Tarr. *The Horse in the City*. Baltimore: Johns Hopkins UP, 2007.

McTaggart, M. F. *A Handbook for Horse Owners*. London: Metheun, 1934.

Miller, Mary E. *Baroness of Hobcaw*. Columbia: South Carolina UP, 2006.

Mitchum, Petrine Day. *Hollywood Hoofbeats*. Irvine, CA: 1-5 Publishing, 2014.

Mooney, Katherine C. *Race Horse Men*. Cambridge: Harvard UP, 2014.

Myres, Sandra L. *Westering Women and the Frontier Experience 1800–1915*. Albuquerque: New Mexico UP, 1982.

Nance, Susan. *Entertaining Elephants: Animal Agency and the Business of the American Circus*. Baltimore: Johns Hopkins UP, 2013.

Nagler, Barney. *The American Horse*. New York: Macmillan, 1996.

Nir, Sarah Maslin. *Horse Crazy: The Story of a Woman and a World in Love with an Animal*. New York: Simon and Schuster, 2020.

Ours, Dorothy. *Man o' War: A Legend Like Lightning*. New York: St. Martin's, 2006.

Peck, William Farley. *History of Rochester and Monroe County, New York*. New York: Pioneer Publishing, 1908.

Pierson, Melissa Holbrook. *Dark Horses and Black Beauties*. New York: Norton, 2000.

Post, Emily. *Etiquette in Society, in Business, in Politics and at Home*. New York: Funk & Wagnalls, 1922.

Prior-Palmer, Lara. *Rough Magic: Riding the World's Loneliest Horse Race*. New York: Catapult, 2019.

Raulff, Ulrich. *Farewell to the Horse*. Translated by Ruth Ahmedzai Kemp. New York: Norton, 2015.

Reynolds, James. *A World of Horses*. New York: Creative Age, 1947.

Riley, Glenda. *Wild Women of the Old West*. Golden, CO: Fulcrum, 2003.

Roach, Joyce Gibson. *The Cowgirls*. Denton: North Texas UP, 1977.

Roosevelt, Theodore. *The Rough Riders*. 1902. New York: Da Capo, 1990.

Scofield, Rebecca. *Outriders: Rodeo on the Fringes of the American West*. Seattle: Washington UP, 2019.

Self, Margaret Cabell. *Horsemanship: Methods of Training*. New York: Barnes, 1952.

Serrano, Richard A. *American Endurance*. Washington, DC: Smithsonian Books, 2016.

Sharpe, Harry. *The Practical Stud Groom*. London: British Bloodstock, 1930.

Shrager, Mark. *Diane Crump*. Guilford, CT: Lyons, 2020.

Sidney, S. *Illustrated Book of the Horse*. 1875. Beverly Hills, CA: Leighton, 2000.

Simon, F. Kevin. *WPA Guide to Kentucky*. Lexington: Kentucky UP, 2014.

Simpson, Henry Clay. *Josephine Clay: Pioneer Horsewoman of the Bluegrass*. Louisville, KY: Harmony House, 2005.

Slout, William L. *Olympians of the Sawdust Circle*. San Bernadino, CA: Borgo, 1998.

Smith, Harry Worcester. *Life and Sport in Aiken*. New York: Derrydale, 1935.

Standiford, Les. *Battle for the Big Top*. New York: Hachette, 2021.

Stansbury, Kathryn B. *Lucille Mulhall*. Self-published, 1985.

172   Selected Bibliography

Swartwout, Annie Fern. *Missie: The Life and Times of Annie Oakley*. Greenville, OH: Coachwhip, 2013.

Thomas, Heidi. *Cowgirl Up!* Billings, MT: TwoDot, 2014.

Twain, Mark. *A Horse's Tale*. 1906. Lincoln: Nebraska UP, 2020.

Wallace, John H. *The Horse of America*. New York: Self-published, 1897.

Weiss, Elaine. *Fruits of Victory: The Woman's Land Army of America in the Great War*. Dulles, VA: Potomac Books, 2008.

Williams, Wendy. *The Horse: The Epic History of Our Noble Companion*. New York: Farrar Straus Giroux, 2015.

Wood-Clark, Sarah. *Women of the Wild West Shows*. Billings, MT: Buffalo Bill Historical Center, 1991.

Index

Amazons, myth of, xv, 2, 3, 12
American Society for the Prevention of Cruelty to Animals, 51
American Red Star Animal Relief, 63
Anmer (horse), 10
Aspinwall, Nan, xvii, 125–29
Astley, Philip, 109
astride riding, 6–7
Atterbury, Mrs. Hoperton, 36

Bagnold, Enid, xvi
Bain, William Charles, 45
Baldwin, Anita, 63
Baldwin, Tillie, 105
Baruch, Belle, 38
Bass, Tom, 46
Beach, Belle, xvi, xix, 15, 27, 33, 39–42, 44–47
Beach, Emily, 38, 40
Beers, Diane L., 54
Belmont Stakes, x
Bergh, Henry, 51
Black Beauty (Sewell), 55, 57
Blackmore, Rachael, ix, x
Black Stallion, The (Farley), x
Blake, Theresa Huntington, 8
Blancett, Bertha, 89
Blodgett, Helen, 30

Bloodgood, Lida Fleitmann, xvii, 2, 30, 32, 33, 36–38, 66, 129
Bloomer, Amelia, 4
Boyd, Anna, 57
Bradley, Joseph, xii
Bradna, Ella, 121
Bradwell, Myra, xii
Brent, Margaret, 16
Brooks, Geraldine, 69
Brown, Velvet, x
Buckner, John, 77, 81–82
Buffalo Bill (William Frederick Cody), 110
Burns, Lucie, 20

Canutt, Kitty, 105
Carpenter, Eliza, xix, 68, 79–80
Carver, Sonora, 134, 138
Carver, William Frank, 135–39
Caton, Kate, 72
Central Park, xx, 1, 6, 24, 25, 26, 30, 33, 99
Chapman, Mary, 11
Cherbonnier, Lucie, 6
Chestick, Dorothy, 1–2
Claire, Alberta, 132–33
Claremont (riding stable), 30
Clay, Josephine, 69–70
Cleveland, Frances, 26

174 Index

Cody, William Frederick. *See* Buffalo Bill
Coolidge, Calvin, 117
Crashaw, Mr. and Mrs., 58
Cribben, Florence, 35, 36
Crosby, Mary B., 71

Daingerfield, Elizabeth, xiv, xvi, 68, 70,
  74–79, 81–86, 92
Davis, Janet, 110
Davison, Emily, 10
Dean, Ada Evans, 71
Demott, Josephine, 121–23
Deuteronomy, 3, 4
Dickel's (riding academy), 30
docking of tails, 56–57
Dog's Tale, A (Twain), 55
Doncaster Model (horse), 42
Down, Alastair, ix
Doyle, Hollie, x
Dreamland, 138
Durland's Riding Academy, 6, 30, 42
Dyson, Mattie, 71

Ehrlich, Mrs. Jacob, 63
Ewing, Ruth, 60

fire horses, 60–61
Forrest, Susanna, 109
French, Arnette, 139
Frontier Days, 105
Furlong, Charles W., 106

Garfield Equestrian Club, 26
Gerken, Carolyn Ridley, 42–44
Gerkendale, 43
Gifford, Mrs. Robert L., 60
Girl and Five Brave Horses, A (Carver), 115
Godiva, Lady, xv, 12, 19
Grand National, ix
Gray Dawn (horse), 19–20
Greene, Ann Norton, 55, 63
Guy, George, 59

Hanna, Mark, 4
Hayes, Brian, ix
Hazard, Martha, 48
Higginbotham, Mary, 126

Higginson, James, 8
Hinkley, Gladys, 13
Holloway, G. F., 134–36
Holloway, J. O., 8
Horse's Tale, A (Twain), 55
Howard, May, 132
Howe, Marie Jenney, xiii

Jennings, Mabel, 6
Johnson, Hilda, 26
Jones, Mary Algood, 50
Jones, Rosalie, 19
Jordan, Jessie, 56

Kane, Elizabeth, xvii, 84–86
Karr, Elizabeth, 28–29
Kayser, Mrs. Charles W., 22
Keeneland Library, xvii
Keller, Helen, xvi, 117
Kelly, William, 64
Kentucky Oaks, x
Kernochan, Eloise, 49
Kincel, Dorothy, 72–3
Knoblauch, May Bookstaver, 15

Ladenburg, Emily, 49
Lady Ellen (horse), 126–29
Lepore, Jill, 12
Letter, Daisy, 49
Letts, Elizabeth, 124
Library of Congress, xvii
Lillie, May, 102
Longworth, Alice Roosevelt, xvi, 18,
  34, 129
Losey, Linda, 124
Loter, Charlotte, 64–65
Lozen, 88
Lumsden, Joan, 13, 19

Madison Square Garden, xvii, 36–39, 46,
  52, 76, 99, 101, 115
Manhattan Saddlery, 24
Man o' War (horse), xvi, 79, 80–83, 85–86
Marantette, Madame (Emma Peek), xvii,
  112, 119–21, 132, 134
Mayo, Margaret, 112
Mayor, Adrienne, 2

Index 175

McCammon, Holly, 12
McShane, Clay, 53, 64
Milholland, Inez, xii, 13, 15, 17–20, 22, 122
Millay, Edna St. Vincent, 18
Mistress Nell (horse), 42
Mulhall, Lucille, xvi, 89, 96–102, 137
Mulhall sisters, xiv
Mullins, Patrick, ix

National Sporting Library, xviii, 141
National Velvet, x, xvi
Neepler, Ida Blake, 16
New York Horse Show, 36
New York Women's League for Animals, 63
North Side Riding Club, 4

Oakley, Annie, xix, 4, 89, 92
O'Leary, Eddie, ix
Oliver, Marian, 131
Olmsted, Frederick Law, 1

Packard, Anna, 59
Paul, Alice, 19, 20
Peek, Myrtle, 119
Pendleton Round-Up, 105–6
Petan, Gertrude, 92
Piepmeier, Alison, 12
Piping Rock Horse Show, 23
Pittsburgh Hippodrome, 139
Ponce de Leon Avenue, 7
Pontifax, Cora, 71
Princess Wenona, 104
Prior-Palmer, Lara, xv
Prix de Diane, x
Proctor, Daysie, 84
Pullan, Tessa, 141

Rasmussen, Ellen, 38
Raulff, Ulrich, x, xvi
Red Star. *See* American Red Star Animal Relief
Reuter-Twining, Diana, 142
Reyher, Rebecca Hourwich, 12
Rice, Grantland, 83
Riddle, Sam, 79, 81
riding accidents, 7–9

Riley, Glenda, 89
Rock Creek Park, 26, 35
Roosevelt, Edith, 34, 35
Roosevelt, Ethel, 34, 35, 36
Roosevelt, Theodore, xvi, 1, 34, 57, 96–97, 102, 131, 132
Root, Mrs. L. B., 60
Russell, Teresa, 95

Schaffter, Mrs. Florian, 56
Schreiber, Caroline, 83–84
Scofield, Rebecca, 88
Sewell, Anna, 55
sidesaddle riding, 2–5
Sisson, E. I., 35
Southworth, E. D. E. N., 55
SPCA (Society for the Prevention of Cruelty to Animals), 57, 61, 64, 65
Sperry Steele, Fannie, 89, 92, 105
Sprague, Ethel Chase, 26
Standiford, Les, 109
Stanton, Elizabeth Cady, xiv
Starr, Belle, 4
Stewart, Marie, 15
Strickland, Mabel, 106–7
Sweeney, Hilary, 64

Taylor, Elizabeth, xvi
Tennyson, Lord Alfred, 19
Thomasville, Georgia, 6
Thompson, Minnie, 102–4
Tinker, Annie, xvi, 5, 13–15
Triangle Shirtwaist Factory, xii
Trickey, Lorena, 107
Tronwig, Dorothy, 59
Twain, Mark, 55, 67

Udall, Madge, 13

Vanderbilt, Mrs. Alfred, 36
Van Hahn, Helen, 25

Wadsworth, Martha Blow, xx, 129–31
Wainwright, Estelle, 112
Walker, Marcialette, 92
Washington Square, 15
Watson, Ella (Cattle Kate), 92–94

176   Index

Wentworth, Rosa, 117–19, 121
Westerberg, Harry, 29
Wilkins, Annie, 124
Wilson, Woodrow, xii, 19

Wirth, May, xvi, xix, 110, 117, 121
Wise, Stephen, 15
workhorse parades, 61, 62–63
World Columbian Exposition, 67, 90–91

Horses in History

Series Editor: James C. Nicholson

For thousands of years, humans have utilized horses for transportation, recreation, war, agriculture, and sport. Arguably, no animal has had a greater influence on human history. Horses in History explores this special human-equine relationship, encompassing a broad range of topics, from ancient Chinese polo to modern Thoroughbred racing. From biographies of influential equestrians to studies of horses in literature, television, and film, this series profiles racehorses, warhorses, sport horses, and plow horses in novel and compelling ways.